Reincarnation Explored

Cover art by *Jane A. Evans*

Reincarnation Explored

John Algeo

*This publication made possible with
the assistance of the Kern Foundation*

The Theosophical Publishing House
Wheaton, Ill. U.S.A.
Madras, India / London, England

The Theosophical Publishing House
306 West Geneva Road
Wheaton, IL 60187

A publication of the Theosophical Publishing House, a department of the Theosophical Society in America.

Library of Congress Cataloging in Publication Data

Algeo, John
    Reincarnation explored.

    "A Quest original"—T.p. verso.
    Bibliography: p.
    Includes index.
    1. Reincarnation. I. Title.
BL515.A42 1987   133.9'01'3   87-40130
ISBN 0-8356-0624-4 (pbk.)

Printed in the United States of America

To the Fellows of the Lodge
near the Beech Tree,
Atlanta, Georgia,
once, now, and future companions

About the Author

John Algeo is professor of English at the University of Georgia, Athens, where he has served as director of the curriculum in linguistics and head of the department of English. He specializes in fantasy literature, the history of the English language, present-day usage, and English grammar. He received both the M.A. and Ph.D. degrees from the University of Florida.

Formerly editor of the journal *American Speech* and director of the commission on the English Language (National Council of Teachers of English), the author has been a consultant for the National Endowment for the Humanities as well as for several university and commercial presses. He served as visiting professor at the University of Erlangen-Nuremberg, Germany, and was recently both a Guggenheim fellow and a Fulbright research scholar at University College London. He is the author or co-author of a number of scholarly books.

Dr. Algeo has been a student of the Ancient Wisdom for many years. He frequently contributes to Theosophical journals and lectures from Theosophical platforms, both in the United States and abroad. He is currently Vice President of the Theosophical Society in America and serves on the editorial advisory committee for Quest Books.

Contents

Preface

Reincarnation is not a subject about which one can be dogmatic, or assume general acceptance of acknowledged fact. If we want to discuss the stratigraphic configuration of the earth's crust or the recipe for making caramel flan, we can go to an expert—a geologist or a chef. They are persons who, by virtue of study and experience, have acquired first-hand knowledge of strata and custards. They are authorities. And everybody will acknowledge that they know what they are talking about. Of course, they may still be wrong: geologists change their minds about what causes mountains to rise, and the best of chefs may have a failed custard from time to time. Nevertheless they are more likely to be right about their special subjects than a nonspecialist would be. Their training and experience mean that we need to pay attention to what they say about their subjects.

THE BASIS OF THIS BOOK

Who is an authority on reincarnation? Who is generally acknowledged to have specialized knowledge about that subject? In fact, there are persons who claim to have, by study and personal experience, special familiarity with the subject. But the knowledge they lay claim to cannot be acquired by following a prescribed course of study at a university or a recipe in a cookbook. It is of a different sort. And therefore it is not generally acknowledged, like knowledge about geology or cooking. In the sense that geologists and chefs are authorities in their fields whose authority is generally accepted, there are no authorities about reincarnation.

Although there are no authorities, there are books aplenty. Recently reincarnation has been given much attention in the press and on television. Books have been published setting forth various sorts of evidence for reincarnation. Other books have been published evaluating and sometimes attempting to refute that evidence. Personal memoirs of prominent persons have appeared explaining the writers' belief in reincarnation. Although it is still widely regarded as an idea that is at least a bit odd, if not decidedly Eastern lunatic fringe, more and more attention is being focused on reincarnation.

So, then, how has anyone the temerity to write another book on this subject for which there are no authorities? And why is another book needed? This book presents no new evidence for or against reincarnation. Instead it gives an overview of the various arguments that have been made, and it also provides a coherent statement of one approach to the subject.

This book gives a theosophical view of reincarnation. The view presented is "a" rather than "the" theosophical view because there are no theosophical dogmas about reincarnation, or any other subject. Indeed, theosophical writers have presented several rather different explanations of how reincarnation works, although they are generally agreed about why it works—its place in the total economy of life. Different descriptions are not to be wondered at since the theosophical approach is to explore diverse viewpoints as partial statements of truth, always assuming that no single statement can express the complete truth of any matter.

PROOF, EXPLANATIONS, AND EVIDENCE

The truth of reincarnation should be an empirical matter subject to investigation and experimentation, but we have no empirical techniques to investigate it satisfactorily. Consequently, in fact, reincarnation is a metaphysical issue—a part of our basic assumptions about how the world works. This book surveys a variety of empirical questions connected with reincarnation, but it approaches all of them with a theosophical worldview, a theosophical metaphysics.

Although ideas about reincarnation cannot be "proven" in the way that we can "prove" ideas about stratigraphy and flan-baking, they can be tested in a variety of ways suitable to the type of idea they are. We can ask whether they provide a satisfactory explanation for the world about us. If reincarnation is a fact, does it explain otherwise puzzling things in life? Is there anything inherently implausible or self-contradictory in the idea? Does it fit in well with other things we know, or believe, to be true about life? Is it a neat, clear idea that appeals to us? Positive answers to such questions are another kind of evidence for reincarnation.

You may object that such evidence would not count for much in a court of law. True. But we are concerned not with legal truth, but rather with intellectual conviction. And it turns out that most of our basic assumptions about life and the world are matters of intellectual conviction that have precisely the kind of evidence mentioned in the preceding paragraph. In the philosophy of science such kinds of evidence are called by high-sounding names like empirical adequacy, self-consistency, systematicity, and simplicity. But what it comes down to is that the bedrock of our belief is a matter of whether an idea fits neatly into a complex of other beliefs that we find workable and satisfying. That is the only kind of evidence we have for the ultimates of life.

The following pages cite evidence and information that have been proffered about reincarnation from a variety of sources. Nothing on these pages is put forth as established fact, but only as a hypothesis about human life. If these ideas have no appeal, if they do not satisfy a sense of order, or if they offend a sense of the plausible, the reader will—and should—reject them. If, however, these ideas are appealing, if they provide plausible and satisfying explanations of at least part of the conundrum of life, the reader may decide to accept them, at least tentatively, to see what their implications are. Those who do so will find that these ideas fit in very well indeed with a number of others, all of which collectively make up what is sometimes called the Wisdom Tradition or, in one of its modern forms, Theosophy.

SOURCES OF THE INFORMATION

The sources of the ideas presented in this little book are various. Partly they come from research by conventionally trained scientists, research that has been made as rigorous as its subject allows. Some of this research has probed the experiences of persons who have nearly died, but who have recovered, bringing back with them an impression of what it is like to die. Other research has explored cases of spontaneous memory, especially among children, of a past life, when the remembered details could be checked for accuracy. Yet other research has investigated cases of induced memory through hypnosis, "past life regression."

Part of the ideas in this book come from a different

sort of research, that by natural or trained clairvoyants who claim to be able to perceive levels or aspects of reality that are not available through normal sensory channels. Edgar Cayce, who gave "life readings" (and several other kinds of "readings") while in a trance state, is one such clairvoyant. Another is Charles Webster Leadbeater, a clergyman who was also a psychic investigator. His research was conducted in full consciousness, but by the use of what he claimed to be powers of perception inherent in all of us, though active only in a few as the result of special training. All such clairvoyant research must be treated gingerly, if not skeptically, not because clairvoyance is fraudulent (though some certainly is), but rather because clairvoyant perception by its very nature is highly personal. It is subject to greater error than normal perception as a result of the nature of the things perceived, as well as the high level of interference from the clairvoyant's own mindset and expectations.

General sources for the subject of this book are the teachings of the religions of India that number reincarnation among their basic doctrines. Those religions include Hinduism, Buddhism, Jainism, and Sikhism. No effort is made to explore in detail the variations in reincarnationism held by those or other religions. Within the general concept of a return to bodily birth in this world, there are various concepts about what part of us is reborn, how rebirth occurs, how soon it happens, what takes place between death and birth, and so on. A comparative study of reincarnationist beliefs is the subject for another book. What appears in the following pages is not the specific doctrine of any religion, but the general concept behind all of them.

A more specific source for the ideas in this book is a tradition of teachings that appear in various forms all over the world and at all periods of human history: the

Wisdom Tradition. In technologically simple cultures such teachings appear as a simple form of shamanism. In intellectually sophisticated cultures they have appeared as Taoism in China, Vedanta in India, Vajrayana in Tibet, Gnosticism in the Classical Mediterranean world, Kabbalism among the Jews, Sufism among the Moslems, and under various other names.

There is a historical connection, a line of cultural transmission, among some of these manifestations of the Wisdom Tradition, but not among all of them. To a considerable extent, its particular expressions are local manifestations of an impulse and a knowledge, a way of looking at the world, that is inherent in the human psyche. That inherent knowledge (something like the contents of Carl Jung's collective unconscious) expresses itself according to the special and variable cultural patterns of diverse times and places, but is recognizably the same in all of them.

Just as in Jungian psychology we can know the nature of an unconscious archetype by studying its manifestations in literature, myth, art, dreams, reveries, and delusions, so we can learn the nature of the underlying Wisdom Tradition by studying its expression in those religious and philosophical movements of the human spirit that have a recognizable affinity with each other. Reincarnation is part of that Wisdom Tradition. By studying the teachings of the historical expressions of the Tradition we can learn something about the reality of reincarnation.

ACKNOWLEDGMENTS

As is true of any work, in the making of this book there are more debts owing than can possibly be repaid or even acknowledged. All the persons who have contributed in one way or another to this book have my deepest gratitude, although they are too many to name. However, a few persons who have contributed specifically cannot go unmentioned: John Kern, who shared both his enthusiasm for making theosophical ideas more widely known and his computer, on which the manuscript was written; Lilian Storey, who made available the resources of the national library of the Theosophical Society in England; and Colyn Boyce, who asked me to fill in for an unexpectedly incapacitated speaker at the Theosophical Society in London and, since I was incompetent in the announced subject, proposed that I talk about reincarnation instead.

Special thanks are due to Dora Kunz and Clarence Pedersen for their helpful comments on the first draft of the manuscript. And my warmest thanks go to several persons whose detailed and perceptive comments have made this a better book than it would otherwise have been: Edward Abdill, Geoffrey Farthing, Virginia Hanson, Joy Mills, Shirley Nicholson, E. Lester Smith, Carl Stillman, and Renée Weber. To the extent that I have not been able to follow all of their suggestions, it is undoubtedly a poorer book than it should be.

And for my wife, Adele, who helped at every stage and without whom nothing would ever get done, there are not words enough.

1

What Is Reincarnation?

A few years ago there was an advertisement for beer that used the slogan: "Live life with gusto—you only go around once!" That slogan is a variation on a theme called *carpe diem*, an expression used by Latin poets and meaning 'seize the day.' The idea is put in various ways, for example, "Eat, drink, and be merry" or "You only live once." But is that right? Do we live only once, or do we live many times? Do we perhaps "go around" life after life?

Reincarnation is the belief that we have not just one life, but many lives, indeed, life after life, right here on this earth. It says that our present life is not the first one we have had here. It says that when our body dies, some part of us will continue to exist for a time without a physical body and then will be drawn back to the physical earth and into a new, developing human body, to start the life cycle over again. In that way we go on, life after life, experiencing, learning, seeking, until we have finished our course on earth and acquired all the wisdom that is to be discovered in this world. Reincarnation is one concept about what happens when we die.

DEATH AND SURVIVAL

An old saying has it that the only things certain in life are death and taxes. But in fact some people manage

1

to avoid taxes. No one avoids death. W. Somerset
Maugham tells a parable about a servant who is in the
marketplace of Bagdad when he sees Death among the
crowd. He is so frightened that he rushes home to his
employer and asks to borrow his horse so that he may
run away from the city—he will go to Samarra, where
Death cannot find him. After lending the horse to his
servant, the employer goes to the marketplace to find
Death, and asks, "Why did you frighten my servant this
morning?" Death answers, "I did not intend to frighten
him; I was merely surprised to see him here in Bagdad
because I have an appointment with him tonight in
Samarra."

Although it is inevitable, death is not necessarily final.
Human beings all over the world, in all places, and as
far as we can tell at all times, have believed that something in us survives death. Not all persons have believed
in survival after death, or believe in it today, but prac-
tically all human cultures have held such a belief. Collectively, humankind has decided that death is not the
end for us.

In some cultures, such as the Egyptian, survival after
death became a central theme of religion and the whole
society: life was organized around death. The burial of
grave goods with a body is an indication of a belief in
survival among primitive peoples. The Neanderthals of
Europe buried their dead folded into a fetal position,
suggesting the expectation that the dead person was to
be born again in another life. And the ideas of survival
and resurrection are central to Christianity. Most religions involve some doctrine of a life after death.

Such a universal belief is quite remarkable and needs
some explanation. Of course, we might decide that
human beings as a species are simply deluded—that our
fear of ceasing to be has led us collectively into a universal delusion. Our belief in survival after death would

then be a defense mechanism to protect ourselves from the unpleasant prospect of our own disappearance. Some people in our own time have reached exactly that conclusion.

On the other hand, we may decide that something believed by all peoples at all times and in all places may just possibly be right. Perhaps human beings collectively have had a perception of reality—have gained a knowledge of things beyond our normal sense perception— and that perception or knowledge is reflected in the general belief of our fellows that somehow we survive the experience of death. The conclusion that we do go on after death is at least as logical as that the whole of humanity has participated in a gigantic mass delusion.

In *A Matter of Personal Survival* Michael Marsh has examined the question of whether a plausible case can be made for personal survival, on purely naturalistic grounds—that is, not considering religious or metaphysical teachings, but just looking logically at the evidence. He concludes that the bulk of the evidence in favor of survival is very substantial and outweighs the evidence against it: "Afterlife," he says, "is not merely a possible future for humankind but a plausible one. Our inquiry justifies a belief in survival" (p. 177).

Quite apart from logic and philosophy, there are also those who claim not just to conclude, but to know: to have experienced death and to remember what it was like and what followed after it. In recent years in the West, a good deal of attention has been given to persons who have had "near-death" experiences—that is, persons who underwent the death experience or something very close to it, but who returned to tell about it. Other persons claim to have extended vision, clairvoyance, by which they can see into the after-death state.

The Wisdom Tradition (or Theosophy) also claims to have information about such matters, which has been

handed down from ancient times and is periodically re-
formulated and stated anew. On the basis of one statement of that tradition, the Tibetans have developed an
ars moriendi—an art of dying—that is integral to their
religion; we call it *The Tibetan Book of the Dead*. More
is said in later chapters about these claims to direct and
traditional knowledge.

If, for the present, we accept the proposition that you
and I will not end with our deaths, but will somehow
go on existing, there are only two general possibilities
about the form that existence will take. On the one hand,
we might exist in a state or world that is different from
the one in which we now live. That is what the dominant religions of the West have generally opted for. Or,
conversely, we might come back into this same world
we now inhabit and take up another body of the same
kind as the one we now have—that is, we might reincarnate. That is the possibility generally favored by
Eastern religious and philosophical traditions.

Reincarnation, although typical of the East, is by no
means limited to that part of the world. Indeed, people all over the globe, East and West, have believed in
reincarnation, and some of those people are considered
in chapter 2. Reincarnation is not really an exotic idea.
Although the concept seemed strange to many people
when the Theosophical Society began to teach it in
Europe and America over a hundred years ago, in fact
there has always been an undercurrent of belief in reincarnation in the West.

Various Concepts of Reincarnation

Many terms have been used to talk about our taking
up another earthly body after death. *Reincarnation* is
the best known and clearest, and so is generally used

here, but some others are given in the appendix at the end of this book.

Just as there are many names for reincarnation and related concepts, there are in fact many varieties of belief in repeated earth lives. These range from simple and naive to highly sophisticated and philosophical. A simplistic notion is that we pop in and out of life as we choose, this time a human being but next time a canary or a horse, or maybe even a mosquito or a rose. That is a popular notion of what reincarnation is, but it is roughly parallel to the naive belief that heaven is a place with golden gates and angels sitting around on cloud puffs playing harps.

Although some varieties of reincarnationism, for example, many schools of Buddhism, do hold that human beings may be reborn as animals, the theosophical tradition maintains that the idea of animal rebirth is symbolic rather than literal. It teaches that reincarnation is part of a vast process of the evolution of consciousness. Just as forms evolve through genetic mutation, the survival of the fittest, and the consequent adaptation of a species to its environment, so consciousness evolves through repeated incarnations in a variety of life forms. And as a giraffe cannot evolve into an oak tree, or a rose bush into a snow flake, so the life energies that make the consciousness of those forms cannot go backwards. Once consciousness has evolved to the human stage, it can never be reembodied in an earlier form.

According to Theosophy, consciousness is a great stream that pours into a variety of channels (the mineral, vegetable, animal, human, and other forms). Just as the water of a river does not flow backward in its channels, but always toward the sea, so consciousness evolves through the lower forms of life, vegetable and animal, through the human stage, and onward to yet higher expressions. Once consciousness has made a quantum leap, by evolving from the animal kingdom to the human, it cannot go back. Once a human, never again any lower form. Of course, humans can act brutishly, and so some religions have used the metaphor of animal births, even though that metaphor maligns animals since they behave naturally, not cruelly.

KARMA AND REINCARNATION

In its philosophical forms, reincarnation is linked with the idea of karma. Karma is the belief that, just as physical laws like gravity and electromagnetism rule the material universe, so moral law rules the universe of consciousness. Although the word *karma* (meaning 'action') is Sanskrit, the idea can be found universally. It is expressed in the Christian scriptures: "Be not deceived; God is not mocked: for whatsoever a man soweth, that shall he also reap" (Galatians 6.7). Karma is the belief that every action we perform has an inevitable, inescapable consequence. Sooner or later we must face up to the consequences of all our actions. If not in this life, we will do so in another.

Like reincarnation, karma is a concept that can be viewed simply and naively, or more philosophically. In its simple form, we may think of it as a cosmic spiritual balance sheet, on which all our good and bad actions are entered, one day to be repaid with the interest due them. Or it is like Santa Claus, who knows whether we've been naughty or nice. In this simple form, karma is reward and punishment.

In much Eastern philosophy, especially Jain and Buddhist, karma is thought of as a burden to be gotten rid of. It is what traps us in this world of pain and suffering and keeps us chained to the treadmill of reincarnation. In this view all karma, whether painful or pleasant, is evil because it binds us to the world of matter. Other Eastern and Western views, especially theosophical ones, are quite different. They associate karma and reincarnation with the concepts of evolution and progress, as the means by which consciousness comes into self-realization.

Viewed maturely, karma is the general principle of moral and spiritual order in the universe. As it relates to us personally, it is not reward and punishment, but challenge and opportunity. The circumstances of our present life are ones we have created or chosen by our actions in past lives. And the way we respond to things in this life will determine what sort of circumstances await us in our next life. Karma is not a fate imposed on us from without; it is the condition by which we exercise free will to determine our lives. And it is the opportunity we have now to choose our future.

Reincarnation and karma are closely linked concepts. According to Theosophy, their interaction is the way consciousness evolves. Karma is the law by which we make ourselves—each of our actions helping to mold our future character and circumstances. Reincarnation is our repeated coming into the world in search of experience—to meet old and make new karma. As we move through time, through the ages of the universe, with these twin motive forces guiding us, we participate in the evolution of conscious life. You and I and the whole human race are only small episodes in that complete evolutionary sweep. But each episode is necessary to the whole story. Each of us is one link in the chain of life, every link of which is indispensable.

AN ANSWER

The question of what reincarnation is can be answered in many ways. On the one hand, it is simply the repeated birth of a soul in new human bodies. On the other hand, it is the means by which consciousness grows and evolves. It is the spiritual equivalent of evolutionary adaptation to an environment. Reincarnation is our opportunity to learn all the lessons this world has to teach. It is our opportunity to enjoy and to suffer, to experience and to sympathize, to grow and to become, to discover what and who we truly are.

2

Who Believes in Reincarnation?

*R*eincarnation is a belief we usually associate with the great religions and philosophies of India—especially those of the Hindus and Buddhists, but also of the Jains and Sikhs. Although belief in reincarnation is pervasive in the traditions of the Indian subcontinent, it is found also throughout the world: in East and West, from ancient times until today, among the famous and the ordinary. It is a view of life and death that is the heritage of anyone who wishes to adopt it.

EASTERN AND WESTERN VIEWS OF HISTORY

Eastern cultures have tended to adopt a cyclical view of world history: that all life proceeds in a spiral, constantly returning—not to exactly the same state as before, but to the same kind of state. In this view, life is like a great square dance, in which dancers weave their way in and out, passing among one another, constantly shifting positions, until at the end of the dance they have all returned to their same relative positions, although the whole pattern of the dancers on the floor may have shifted. A cyclical view of life naturally encourages a belief in reincarnation. If we return to birth repeatedly, human life is part of the great cosmic dance—it fits in, it harmonizes and makes sense.

The West, on the other hand, until recently has been dominated by a straight-line view of history. Put simply, the orthodox view in Christianity is that God created the world out of nothing, and the world then proceeded under the Old Dispensation given out by the Patriarchs and the Prophets until Christ came to give the New Dispensation, under which the Church looks after things until the Second Coming and the end of the world. Start to finish, world history is thought of as a straight line, like a highway crossing the plains with no curves and nothing to block the sight of its disappearance at the horizon. Such a view is not hospitable to reincarnation.

Moreover, when secular historians in the West constructed worldviews of human culture, they kept the straight-line approach inherited from the Church. And so secular history was seen as consisting of ancient Classical civilization, followed by the Middle Ages, which gave way to the Renaissance and modern times, including the growth in our own age of science and technology. This view was meant to be an alternative to the religious one, but it used the same metaphor and had the same flaws.

One of the problems with the straight-line view of human history, whether sacred or secular, is that it ignores everybody who happens to be off the line—and in both straight-line versions that turns out to be most of humanity. Those who are not Jews or Christians and those who are not Europeans just do not fit on the line, and so are ignored, even though they are the majority of humankind. The straight-line view is parochial and ethnocentric.

To be sure, some Westerners have regarded the world in a more cyclical way. Some modern physicists think that the universe expands and contracts alternately throughout all time—an oscillating universe that is inherently cyclical. The historian Arnold Toynbee, a devout Christian, believed that all history can be seen as a series of rises and falls of human cultures, a vast pattern of cycles. And in earlier times many in the West have held a cyclical view of life that is hospitable to a belief in reincarnation. Indeed, from the earliest days of Western and Christian civilization, a belief in reincarnation has been widely held as an alternative to the one-life doctrine of institutional Christianity.

CHRISTIANITY, THE WISDOM TRADITION, AND REINCARNATION

The theologian and scholar Geddes MacGregor has argued that reincarnation is by no means incompatible with Christianity. He proposes that it offers a reasonable interpretation of the Christian afterlife and of the concept of purgatory—the doctrine that we must, in some world, work off the consequences of our evil deeds. He also argues that reincarnation has formed part of the informal, noncreedal belief of some Christians in the past and that it conflicts with nothing in the core of Christian doctrine.

The earliest Christians were preoccupied with the need to spread the gospel before the end of the world, which they expected to come any day. Consequently, they had little time for speculating about the next life. Once, however, it became clear that Christ was not going to return during the first generation of Christians, they began to think of what the future might hold. Knowledge about reincarnation was distributed over the whole Mediterranean world at the time, so the early Christians could not have been unaware of it. Such ideas had been taught by Pythagoras and Plato, and were held by many Greek and Roman philosophers.

The Gospels themselves contain evidence that reincarnation was accepted as, at least, a possibility by early Christians. One story tells of the disciples being troubled by the justice of a man who was born blind. They asked Christ, "Master, who sinned—this man or his parents—that he should be born blind?" That question makes no sense if the disciples supposed that each human soul was created with its earthly body. It makes sense only if they supposed it is possible for us to have lived a life before the present one, a life in a world like this one, where we may sin and thus set up consequences that we must meet in a later life.

One of the intellectual giants among the Fathers of the Church, the third-century Origen, certainly taught that souls exist before being born in this life, and he probably taught a form of reincarnation. We cannot be sure of the exact form of his teaching because his writings were censored and expurgated by both his enemies and his friends (who wanted to protect him against persecution). The teachings of Origen, himself a gentle and holy man, were caught up in the rancor of church politics, so that a hundred and fifty years after his death, his teachings in general were first condemned by a church council. The early church councils and the political machinations that accompanied them were so confused, however, that it is not certain that the doctrine of reincarnation was ever declared unsuitable for Christians.

Some Christians, albeit persecuted ones, certainly went on holding to a belief in reincarnation. The most famous of them were the Albigensians or Cathars, an eleventh-century group in southern France and northern Italy, who were also vegetarians and were opposed to the domination of the laity by the church hierarchy. The Albigensian devotion to harmlessness, pacifism, chastity, and freedom from clerical tyranny earned them the admiration of the masses and the lasting enmity of the clergy. When attempts to convince them of the error of their ways were unsuccessful, the Church set about persecuting them through the inquisition, and by the end of the fourteenth century had almost exterminated them.

The Albigensian community expressed the Wisdom Tradition, whose beginnings are lost in the mists of prehistoric time and which has continued to be embodied in other forms down through the ages. Albigensian teachings, including reincarnation, were not original with that group, and did not end with them. Indeed similar doctrines are to be found in both Judaism and Islam—the other Western "religions of the Book." In Judaism, reincarnation features as a teaching within the tradition of Kabbalism and one of its modern expressions, Hasidism. In these Jewish traditions, reincarnation is known by the Hebrew term *gilgul*. In Islam reincarnation is taught among the Sufis, who claim to know the esoteric meaning of the Koran.

Although reincarnation is typically espoused by the mystical and esoteric branches of the major Western religions—the Albigensians, Kabbalists, and Sufis—not all churchmen have rejected it. Maud Gonne was an activist in Irish politics and was the inspiration of some of William Butler Yeats's greatest poems. In her autobiography she tells that a French priest once asked her why she was not a Catholic. She answered, "Because I believe in reincarnation; I believe I have lived in this beautiful world before. Some of the people I meet are people I have already known so well that I know the things they are going to say." The priest, a wise and understanding man, answered, "The soul comes from God and returns to God when purified, when all things will become clear; and who can tell the stages of its purification? It may be possible some souls may work out their purification on this earth" (261-62).

Similarly, Quincy Howe, Jr., has written a thoughtful

study, *Reincarnation for the Christian,* in which he examines ideas about the subject from both the Indian and Platonic traditions and offers a defense of them in the light of the theological and metaphysical assumptions of orthodox Christianity. His work and that of Geddes MacGregor, referred to earlier, are evidence that some Christian theologians today are willing to give sympathetic consideration to the idea of reincarnation.

Famous People and Literature

All through the years, reincarnation has been taught by certain groups, often those who have stood apart from the dominant culture of the West, and by some individuals, often quite well-known ones. Giordano Bruno, the sixteenth-century philosopher who was burnt at the stake for his liberal views, held a doctrine of reincarnation, and so did the modern Italian patriot Giuseppe Mazzini. Writers and artists who have believed in reincarnation include Johann Wolfgang von Goethe, Ralph Waldo Emerson, Henry David Thoreau, Louisa May Alcott, Edward Bulwer-Lytton, Richard Wagner, Dante Gabriel Rossetti, William Ernest Henley, Sir Rider Haggard, Sir Arthur Conan Doyle, Rudyard Kipling, Jack London, Gustav Mahler, Leo Tolstoy, J. B. Priestley, John Masefield, William Butler Yeats, Salvador Dali, and many others. The British Prime Minister David Lloyd George was a reincarnationist, as were Napoleon Bonaparte, Thomas Edison, Henry Ford, and German philosophers like Lessing, Herder, and Schopenhauer. The lists could go on and on.

Sylvia Cranston, first in collaboration with Joseph Head and later with Carey Williams, has produced three books detailing the widespread belief in reincarnation among the peoples of the world and collecting quotations from famous persons and works about reincarnation. These books make surprising reading for anyone who has thought that only kooks and weirdos accept the idea of rebirth. Reincarnation is not exotic or impractical. The idea has been held, and is held even today, by the famous and the unfamous alike, all over the world.

A measure of the domestication of reincarnation is its use as a theme in popular forms of entertainment. In the mid 1960s, a hit Broadway musical was *On a Clear Day You Can See Forever*, by Alan J. Lerner. The play concerns a psychotherapist using posthypnotic suggestion to treat the compulsive behavior of Daisy, a young woman who is awkward and suffers from acute feelings of inferiority but is also psychically very gifted (she talks to her plants, which grow phenomenally for her). In the course of her treatment, the therapist accidentally regresses her to a past incarnation, when she was a beautiful and supremely self-confident eighteenth-century woman named Melinda.

The therapist is stunned by the implications of the regression and fascinated by the personality of Melinda, with whom he falls in love—although he has no respect or regard for the wretchedly ordinary Daisy. Daisy, however, is flattered by the attention the therapist gives her and falls in love with him, only to resent bitterly the fact that he cares only for the subliminal Melinda. Like all good musicals, this one ends happily, with Daisy integrating those qualities of Melinda that the doctor (and the audience) admire, without losing her own identity.

What is noteworthy about this musical play is that it treats reincarnation seriously as the hinge on which the plot turns. As Lerner remarked in an interview on the play, "Somebody asked me if I thought *On a Clear Day You Can See Forever* was a fantasy because it touched on the possibility of reincarnation, and I said,

'Well, no, not to five hundred million Indians it isn't.' "
(Stewart 100).

A contrasting work of fiction is the novel *The Rein-carnation of Peter Proud*, a mystery thriller about a young man who discovers he is the reincarnation of a man who had been murdered by his wife after a violent quarrel and who now falls in love with a girl—his daughter from the previous life—only to be murdered again under the same circumstances by the girl's mother, his former wife. This titillating combination of murder and pseudo incest was filmed, thus becoming another channel for making reincarnation more widely known and less exotic, if not less spooky to the cinema-going public.

A recent independent film with a reincarnation theme is *Return*, written and directed by Andrew Silver. The recipient of a variety of film-festival awards, it is also available in video cassette format. Silver's well-made film shows that reincarnation and the paranormal continue as popular themes for mass entertainment.

Increasingly now, open acknowledgment of reincarnation is passing from fiction to fact. Public persons like the actress Shirley MacLaine are declaring their belief in it. MacLaine's autobiographical books *Out on a Limb* and *Dancing in the Light* have done much to make reincarnation more widely known. Indeed those books and the television production of *Out on a Limb* have helped to make reincarnation a fashionably glitzy subject.

Fictional treatments of reincarnation and its espousal by Hollywood celebrities do not make it true, but they do show that an idea which was once bizarre is on its way to becoming commonplace. The success of such popular treatments bears witness to a great hunger for reassurance about life after death and to an openness by millions of people to considering reincarnation. That is new in our culture.

EVERYMAN AND EVERYWOMAN

Private persons are also increasingly acknowledging a belief in reincarnation. A Gallup Youth Survey published in 1985 revealed that 27 percent of the teenagers polled in the United States "accept the eastern religious concept of reincarnation, that the soul does not go to a heaven or hell but passes on to live in another being" *(Athens* [Georgia] *Banner-Herald,* 20 Mar. 1985, C-3). The fact that more than a quarter of the new generation of Americans should announce a belief in reincarnation suggests that in the coming years the old idea that it is a teaching associated with the East and foreign to the West, or at least an oddity, will have to be abandoned.

Popular acceptance of reincarnation is more widespread than one might have imagined. Gallup surveys made earlier in the 1980s and reported in Gallup and Proctor's *Adventures in Immortality* (130, 176-78) show that 23 percent of the adults polled believe in reincarnation. The highest proportion of those who espouse the idea of rebirth are young and urban; the lowest proportion are older and rural. Those demographic facts suggest that belief in reincarnation is likely to become increasingly frequent and increasingly influential. It is the wave of the future.

Who believes in reincarnation? Quite a lot of people do: writers and musicians, politicians and philosophers, inventors and industrialists, show-biz people and the man and woman in the street. Christians do, as do Jews and Moslems, as well as Hindus and Buddhists. The chances are quite good that someone living on your block does. It is not unlikely that someone in your house does. Maybe even you.

3

Can Reincarnation Explain Life's Puzzles?

Why do so many people accept reincarnation as a fact, or at least as a likelihood? What are the grounds for believing that we have repeated lives on earth? To be sure, many people, particularly Hindus and Buddhists, believe in reincarnation because they grew up in a culture that accepts reincarnation as a fact of life. That is an unthinking acceptance of an idea.

However, today especially, many persons outside the traditional "reincarnation cultures" are adopting the idea and making it their own. Why are those people persuaded by it? There are reasons of two kinds for accepting any idea as true. One is that the idea provides a reasonable explanation for things we have observed or otherwise know to be true. The other is that there is tested evidence supporting the idea.

For example, we believe that the law of gravity exists. One reason for our belief is that it explains reasonably why the people on the other side of the world don't fall off. Another reason is that we can perform a simple experiment by holding an apple out a second-story window and letting go of it; if gravity is a fact, it should fall—and it does.

In this chapter, we take a look at one of those two grounds for belief—how reincarnation explains life's puzzles. After considering some objections in the following chapter, in chapters 5–8 we examine the other ground for belief—the kinds of testable evidence that have been proposed. The various reasons that have been advanced for believing in reincarnation are not all equally convincing; for some of life's puzzles, there are certainly other and better explanations, but here are seven typical reasons that have been proposed.

DÉJÀ VU

Most people have had the experience of apparently remembering a place or a person where they had never been or whom they had never seen before. It is a curious sensation. You will be walking along, carrying on a conversation, and then suddenly be overpowered by the sensation that you have been in just that place or had just that conversation with the same person before. It usually lasts only a moment or two and then fades, leaving you in the ordinary world, puzzled by what has just happened. Some people have the experience often as children, but find that it fades as they mature.

The experience of having "been there before" is often called by the French term *déjà vu*, literally 'already seen.' There is an alternative term for the experience that is derived from Greek and therefore sounds more scientific: *paramnesia*, literally 'alongside memory.' Psychologists offer a variety of explanations for this curious experience, but it has been suggested that reincarnation is also a possible one. In déjà vu we may have a fleeting but real memory of a place, person, or experience we encountered before, but in a prior life.

Déjà vu is a weak argument for reincarnation. It is a somewhat stronger argument for what the German philosopher Friedrich Nietzsche called "eternal recurrence" (see the appendix). However, there are simpler explanations. Déjà vu may be only a trick of psychological perception, or it may be a momentary tapping into the memory of nature, called the "akashic records" (chapter 6).

PREDISPOSITIONS

More generalized and diffuse than déjà vu is the predisposition we all have in favor of or against certain things. Most of us have irrational likes and dislikes: we react with spontaneous fear, or we form instant friendships. We meet someone for the first time, but it seems that we are old friends who have come back together. Or something quite innocuous, like crossing bridges, may evoke a sense of panic in us. There seems to be no logical explanation for such reactions; they just pop up.

Reincarnation explains such predispositions by saying that they are our dimly remembered responses to things, people, and events of past lives. The new acquaintance who seems like an old friend may be just that—a very old friend from lives gone by. The irrational fear of crossing a bridge may echo some traumatic experience—an accident or a battle—that we took part in on another bridge in another lifetime. Perhaps what seem to be instinctive reactions are really our sensitivity to our own past.

HISTORICAL PATTERNS

Something like individual predispositions can take place on a gigantic scale, involving whole peoples and cultures and stretching through history. The English-speaking peoples of modern Britain and America are in some ways similar to the citizens of ancient Rome. There is the same growth from small provincial beginnings, the same building up of a far-flung empire incorporating diverse peoples and cultures, the same combination of military might and commercial acumen, the same excellence in engineering of buildings and roads, and so on. Throughout history, there seem to be times when one people or historical period mirrors the cultural patterns of another people or period. There are repetitive patterns in the history of nations.

It has been suggested that such apparent historical repetitions can be explained by the wholesale reincarnation in one nation and at one time of souls who had lived together in a prior historical period. Students of reincarnation say that we are not reborn haphazardly; when we are ready to be reborn, we do not just plunk down in whatever body happens to be available. Rather we are drawn to people with whom we have lived before. If that is so, then it is not surprising that souls should tend to "clump together," to be reborn in the same time and place as those with whom they have formed past-life ties.

In that case, modern Anglo-America would be like Rome because Englishmen and Americans are Romans reborn, with the same virtues and the same vices, but a new chance to do things better.

INDIVIDUAL DIFFERENCES

One of the remarkable things about human beings is the propensity we have to be different. Two children of the same parents, raised in the same household, may turn out to be quite unlike each other. The environment and the heredity of both children may be the same, but they turn out to be different.

An American professor once told a story about his daughter, who had done something to annoy him. After he had soundly berated her for her shortcomings and asked her why she had behaved so badly, she looked up at him and sighed, "Which do you suppose it is, Daddy, environment or heredity?" In Western culture we

tend to think that everything can be explained by those
two factors—nurture and nature. We suppose that we
are what we are entirely because of the genes we inherit
from our ancestors or because of the circumstances of
our education and life. And because of that dichotomous
explanation of human behavior, the young girl thought
she had her father in a corner. Whatever she had done
wrong was due to either the heredity she acquired from
him or the environment he had provided. It clearly
wasn't her fault.

Dichotomies, however, are often false. For every two
partially true possibilities, there is usually a third. And
so it is with environment and heredity. If reincarnation
is a fact, in addition to those two factors as explanations
of our character and behavior, there is a third. To be
sure, we are what we are because of the genes we inherit from our ancestors and because of the pressures
of the world around us. But other factors are the inclinations and predispositions we have developed life after
life. We are who and what we are now because of what
we have done in past lives. The Buddhist technical term
for those inclinations and predispositions we bring with
us from former existences is *skandhas*. The skandhas are
the fruits of our actions in all our earlier incarnations.

Extreme cases resulting from the influence of the skandhas are the genius and the idiot savant. Genius, or exceptional and original ability, often manifests very early
in life. Mozart was playing the harpsichord at three,
composing music at four, and touring as a performer
at six. Similarly, Haydn played and composed at six, and
Mendelssohn at nine. Coleridge was reading the Bible
at three, and John Stuart Mill began the study of Greek
at the same age, by the time he was eight having read
Xenophon, Herodotus, and Plato. Tennyson and Goethe
were writing poetry when they were eight, and Lope
de Vega dictated verses at the age of five, before he could
write. As soon as they learned how to write, Charlotte

Brontë and her sisters and brother were composing and acting out plays. Sonja Henie was the figure-skating champion of Norway at the age of ten, and world champion at fifteen. Norbert Wiener entered college at eleven, and had earned a doctorate from Harvard by the time he was eighteen. Environment and heredity clearly play a part in such precocious manifestation of abilities, but they do not explain it.

Other geniuses begin slowly and then later manifest their extraordinary talents. Albert Einstein and Winston Churchill were regarded as very ordinary pupils when they were children, not particularly bright, but Churchill became the best known Prime Minister England has ever had, and Einstein's ideas revolutionized physics, with profoundly practical consequences. A theoretical genius like Einstein or a practical genius like Thomas Alva Edison defies explanation. It is true that Edison has been quoted as saying that genius is one part inspiration and nine parts perspiration, but inspiration still needs explanation, and so does the determination underlying the perspiration.

A very strange condition is that of the idiot savant (a French expression meaning 'learned ignorant person'), a mentally retarded person who has phenomenal ability in some one activity. A British television program of 1987 showed three boys, all severely retarded in their learning ability, autistic (that is, pathologically turned inward and withdrawn from reality), brain-damaged, and with crippling speech problems. Yet each boy possessed some remarkable ability that could hardly be duplicated by normal persons.

One boy had a nearly perfect ear-memory for music. He was unable to read music, but he could hear even the most difficult composition and reproduce it on the piano with nearly perfect accuracy. His musical memory was said to be at the level of Mozart. Another was a calendar-calculator. Given the date of any year, past or future, he could tell the day of the week on which that date would fall—or vice versa, he could spiel forth a list of years on which a given date, say March 18th, would fall on any particular day of the week, such as Tuesday. Moreover, he was able to produce this information faster than a mathematician using a calculating machine could arrive at it. The third boy could produce detailed and highly accurate architectural drawings of professional draftsman quality after having studied a building for only a few minutes.

A possible explanation of genius and child prodigy and the extraordinary ability of the idiot savant is that such persons show the effect of abilities built up over a series of lives devoted to one subject, such as music or science. The environment and heredity have to be right for genius to manifest itself (and differences in those factors may explain why some extraordinarily talented persons are child prodigies and others are mature geniuses). In the theosophical view, the painful retardation of the idiot savant is a karmic limitation that may be but is not necessarily connected with the exceptional ability. Environment and heredity cannot fully explain either extraordinary talent or extraordinary limitations. The person's skandhas, the surviving effects of past-life actions, are a logical explanation of both conditions.

CYCLICITY

All about us we see cycles in nature and in human life: the cycles of day and night, of the phases of the moon, of the tides, of the seasons of the year, of sunspots, of ice ages, of the precession of the equinoxes, of the expansion and contraction of the universe itself, which some cosmologists propose; and on the personal side, cycles of the heartbeat and pulse, of breathing, of temperature fluctuation, of sleeping and waking, of hunger, of menstruation, of all biorhythms. All nature seems to move in patterned repetitions.

If analogy is a valid form of reasoning, we would expect cycles of life and death as well. Reincarnation proposes that the experiences of birth and death are just two points in another natural cycle. Scientists have been searching for a grand unified field theory, which would allow them to subsume all the known laws governing matter under a single general principle. The desire for, and the belief that there must be, a single explanatory principle for things is an ingrained characteristic of the human mind. It is therefore not surprising that, seeing so many cycles about us, we should expect to find cyclicity in our personal experience of life and death.

With regard to the cyclical aspect of reincarnation, we should keep in mind that *death* is an ambiguous word in English. It stands for both an event and a state in one half of the cycle, whereas we have different words (*birth* and *life*) for the corresponding event and state of the other half. The accompanying diagram may help to clarify this distinction.

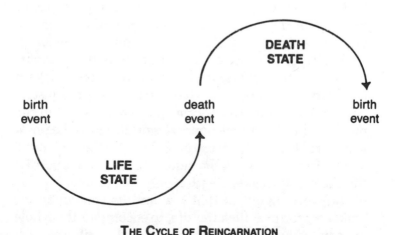

DEATH STATE

birth event   death event   birth event

LIFE STATE

THE CYCLE OF REINCARNATION

Our language leads us to think that personal existence is a three-termed and unrepeatable experience: birth-life-death. But if reincarnation is a fact, it is really a four-termed, recurring experience, as shown in the diagram. The event of birth is the beginning of our state of life; the event of death ends the life state but also begins the (after-)death state, which in turn is ended by a new birth event. We should not allow ourselves to be trapped by the limitations of the language we speak, by what has been called "the prison house of language." The way a given language reports reality is not necessarily the way reality is.

THE QUESTION OF JUSTICE

One of the perennial concerns of human beings has been that of the existence of justice in the world. How is it that the wicked prosper and the virtuous suffer? Why is an innocent baby born with a malformed body? What brings misfortune and pain to a good person? In Judeo-Christian terms, if God is both good and all-powerful, why does he permit evil and unmerited suffering to exist?

Reincarnationism maintains that the appearance of injustice in the world is a consequence of our limited knowledge and vision. If, instead of one lifetime only, we could see the whole series of an individual's incarnations, with the working out of karma across the chain of lifetimes, we would see that perfect and strict justice governs all events. Disorder no more holds sway in the moral realm than in the physical world. Just as the physical world is ruled by cause and effect, so the inviolable law of karma governs the results that follow upon all the choices we make. Death is only a brief interruption in the working out of that law and its consequences, which stretch over life after life, to encompass the whole of an individual's existence in this and all possible worlds.

If you are running a small business, you do not expect to show a profit each day. On some days expenditure will be greater than income—you may pay large bills to restock your shelves, or you may have few customers. But the imbalance of that day does not mean you have to close your doors immediately and declare bankruptcy. It is necessary only that the books be in the black over a long period of many days. So according to the Wisdom Tradition our karmic books do not balance at the end of each lifetime, but only over a long period of many lives.

For some persons, reincarnation is the only satisfactory explanation of the apparent injustices of life. If one assumes, as religions generally have, that justice pervades the universe, it is hard to avoid the conclusion that reincarnation is a logical necessity. Of course, other persons deny the existence of justice in the cosmic order and say that the expectation of it is merely wish-fulfillment and that religion is the opiate of the people. That metaphysical position is, however, no more logical than its contrary, that perfect justice rules the world. And the latter is pragmatically a better basis for living.

MEANING IN LIFE

Perhaps the greatest appeal of reincarnation for many persons is the effectiveness with which it explains the purpose and goal of life. One lifetime is clearly not enough to learn everything earth has to teach us. One lifetime is not enough to experience the full range of joy and bittersweet sorrow that life has to offer. Repeated lives on earth give us a chance to catch up in our next lifetime on what we have missed during this one. They are the promise that we will eventually have an opportunity to experience the full range of life's possibilities and thereby to develop our full potential.

The doctrine of a single lifetime for each individual leaves us as small, lost beings in the midst of an immense and radically foreign, even antagonistic universe. In this view, we are brief flickers of light in the darkness, momentary sparks lost in the depths of boundless space. The teaching of reincarnation holds that we are part of a great, ordered plan of physical-intellectual-spiritual evolution, stretching back to the primordial beginnings of things and moving forward to a final state of perfection.

The notion of immortality and "the life of the world to come" is central to traditional Christian belief, yet is very unclear. One theologian has called it "the most confused aspect of Christian theology" (MacGregor, *Reincarnation as a Christian Hope*, ix). Many Christians have regarded the traditional concepts of life after death—limitless punishment in hell or endless hosannas in heaven—with restrained enthusiasm. The truth is that conventional notions about life after death do not make of it a very attractive or sensible prospect. Reincarnation makes sense of the idea of immortality. If we are to live again after this life, what more probable place to do so than right here where we have lived before? And under what more likely circumstances should we live than those we ourselves have generated in the past? The possibilities before us in this world are manifold. Reincarnation means we will have the opportunity to sample them all and to finish what we have started.

Reincarnation explains many of life's puzzles—both small and great. The fact that it does explain such things is not proof that it is true, of course. But the explanation it offers is a pragmatic reason for accepting it as real. Next, however, we turn to objections that can be raised to the likelihood of reincarnation and to the kinds of verifiable evidence that have been offered for it.

4

What Are the Objections?

The idea of reincarnation is often met with an irrational rejection. Indeed those who most pride themselves
on being rational thinkers may reject it out of hand, with
an emotional intensity that suggests the idea is a threat-
ening challenge to preconceptions and prejudices. If reincarnation is true, a great many other commonly held
notions about the world will have to be reexamined and
doubtless revised too. Reincarnation is thus a challenge
to several commonly held worldviews, religious and
secular.

The threat which reincarnation seems to offer to close-
minded theories, whether fundamentalist Christian or
dogmatic materialist, is met by a number of arguments
against it. Certain objections are thought to be decisive,
although they are in fact nothing of the kind. Among
them are our lack of memory of former lives, the population explosion, and a variety of other responses.

Lack of Memory

One of the first objections to reincarnation is that, if
we have had past lives, we ought to remember them.
That objection is not very well thought out, however.
For one thing, it assumes that we do not remember past

lives, and that is by no means certain. It is quite possible that all of us remember our past lives, at least in a
general way, by the inclinations and abilities we bring
with us from them. In addition, some people may remember them in quite specific ways. A later chapter will
deal in more detail with how we remember past lives
and what we remember about them.

There are other weaknesses to the objection of lack
of memory. If what we do not remember never happened, most of us were never born and never had an
infancy, the telephone number I had ten years ago never
existed, and the bill I put in my coat pocket to pay yesterday is a figment of my wife's imagination. Memory is
notoriously unreliable. Not only do we regularly forget
things that happened, we also sometimes remember
things that never occurred. I have a letter to write, so
while shaving in the morning I plan what I will say in
it and then am distracted by other activities of the day.
Some weeks later, I get a complaint that I have not
answered my correspondent's last letter. "But I did
answer it," I object, "I remember quite clearly what I
said!" Memory is bad evidence.

To remember all our past lives would, in fact, be impossible. A perfect and complete memory for the events
of even this life would be a curse. A total recall of the
trivia of everyday events would be a monstrous clutter-
ing of the mind. Forgetfulness can be a blessing. It is
also a necessity if we are to function effectively day to
day—what we forget is as important as what we remember. If that is true of a single lifetime, how much truer
is it of a series of lives, stretching into the distant past.

If we remembered even the most important things
about our last (let us say) twenty lives, what would that
mean? There would be twenty identities, forty parents,
twenty or more spouses, twenty sets of offspring (perhaps
sixty or a hundred in all), twenty or more occupations,
twenty or more languages, twenty varieties of custom

and obligation, and so on. And how many regrets would there be? How many conflicts of loyalty? How many senses of obligation? How could we keep them all straight and separate from the events of this life? If I knew that my daughter or son of two lives ago is my wife or husband in this life, would that not cause some confusion in my relationship? And if I have changed sex from time to time, as reincarnationists claim, would memories of former sex roles not interfere in this life? How could we cope with such diverse memories? Nature, in her wisdom, wipes the slate clean of specific memories for most of us at the beginning of each new life. We need a fresh start.

In fact, we should not expect specific memories to be carried over from one life to the next. According to Theosophy, in each life we develop a new personality, which has its basis in the physical body of that incarnation. Our brain may not be where memories are stored (memory is in fact a great mystery), but the brain is doubtless involved with the process of storing and tapping into memory. When our brain has ceased to function and our body has dissolved into its components, our personality ceases to exist also. Clairvoyants report that the personality does not long survive the death of the body, so neither do the specific memories linked to it. What carries over from one incarnation to another are general abilities, propensities, and karmic impulses—those factors called the *skandhas* (chapter 3). The question of what reincarnates is considered more fully in chapter 8. Suffice it to say here that it is not the personality—which is made anew in each lifetime—and so neither is it the memory associated with the personality.

THE POPULATION EXPLOSION

Another objection frequently voiced is that the population explosion precludes reincarnation. In 1973 the world's population was estimated to be 3,860,000,000. If the population increased by just 2 percent a year, it would double in 35 years. Where do all those souls come from?

The particular figures are not important; the principle of increasing population is the point. However, it is worth noting that estimates of the current population of the earth are just that—estimates. We do not actually know how many human beings are on our planet now, and we certainly don't know how many were on it 2000 years ago, or 1,000,000 years ago. The further back in time we go, the less certain are our estimates of the size of the human population.

The assumption that we have had a steadily increasing human population through the millennia is based on such evidence as known remains, bones and artifacts, and estimates of the number of people that could be supported on a given area of land in hunting and gathering cultures. It is certainly likely that our present population is the largest the earth has ever supported at one time. It is possible, however, that the present-day increase is a temporary fluctuation rather than part of a long-term trend.

Projections of the size of the earth's population into the past are uncertain, and those into the future are very unreliable. In considering population growth in relation to reincarnation, we must answer a variety of questions. For example, how many "souls" are there in the pool of those being reincarnated? Has the average life span always been what it is today? And is the time between incarnations a constant figure, or can it vary? The density of the incarnate population will vary greatly if such factors fluctuate.

Those who cite the population explosion as an argument against reincarnation usually suppose that rebirth takes place almost immediately after death, whereas the theosophical tradition is that a long time normally elapses between incarnations. The exact length of time is said to vary greatly, ranging from a few years to a "kalpa," that is, a period of millions of years. Either of those extremes would be exceptional, however, and for most persons the time between incarnations has been said to vary from a few hundred to a few thousand years—the exact time depending on the quality of the incarnation and the availability of a suitable birth opportunity.

The estimate in the preceding paragraph was first published about a century ago. More recent investigations, such as those of the psychic Edgar Cayce and those made through hypnotic regression and research into cases of spontaneous past-life memories (discussed in chapters 6–8), suggest a much shorter interval. It may be that as the tempo of modern life is speeding up, so is the tempo of the death state.

There is no reason to suppose that the interval between lives is a fixed period—a kind of invariable natural law. On the contrary, we would expect it to vary just as life spans do, and the average length may well vary greatly, depending upon the circumstances of the world and the evolution of consciousness. In a world with more opportunities for experience available, we should expect an intensified quest for that experience. If life offers more possibilities, we should expect a greater demand for them.

In the past hundred years, the world has changed more in the circumstances of human life than during the preceding hundred thousand. Transportation, communication, housing, medicine, science, manufacturing, literacy, education, and many other features of life have undergone such changes as would hardly have been imaginable a few generations ago. When many of us were children, the idea of human beings standing on the moon was science fiction. Today it is science fact.

From the standpoint of reincarnation, the explanation of the population explosion is fairly obvious. Think of a large pool of individuals reincarnating during a time in the Earth's history when conditions are relatively stable. They reincarnate infrequently, the pull of new experiences being weak. Then, for whatever reason, conditions alter radically. A new social world with vastly increased possibilities for human experience comes into existence. The desire for new experiences is accordingly intensified, and the reincarnating individuals come back into birth much more frequently and after significantly shorter periods between lives. The result is a population explosion.

Think of a movie house that shows the same film for six months at a stretch. People do not rush to see it, because they know they have plenty of time. Then the management begins to change the program every week and to bring in first-run films. With only a week to see the films, patrons come more often and attendance rises dramatically, although the population of the town has not increased. We live in a world of single-week, first-run films. It is hardly surprising that business is booming.

At any given time there may be far more individuals out of incarnation than in. The present population explosion is, in that case, an indication that our time is appropriate for a great many individuals to come into birth. So more are incarnating than usual, with a consequent reduction in the time between incarnations.

To offer the population explosion as an objection to reincarnation also supposes that our Earth is a closed system—that no new incarnating individuals ever appear on our planet. It is true that the theosophical tradition holds that the evolutionary development of human souls from the animal kingdom ended ages ago in our evolutionary cycle. But it also holds that life exists throughout the cosmos, with intelligent life of the human stage on many planets of our galaxy. We do not know enough about the cosmic economy to say whether our planet might have an influx of lives from other globes. But if it should, that too could account for the observed population explosion. In any case, that perceived explosion is no sound argument against reincarnation.

OTHER OBJECTIONS

Some people dismiss reincarnation simply because it seems to them to be a far-out idea—something suggestive of Eastern cults and pop gurus running a religious scam. But as chapter 2 shows, there is nothing disreputable or unusual about the concept. It has been held by a wide variety of persons and groups, in both the East and the West. To dismiss an idea merely because it is unfamiliar is provincial and unworthy of thoughtful persons.

Other people reject reincarnation because the idea does not appeal to them. They do not like the prospect of having to return to this world time after time. Whether reincarnation is a depressing prospect or an exciting one depends on us and on how we approach it. So whether the concept is attractive or repulsive tells us something about ourselves, rather than anything about reincarnation. Our reaction to it is irrelevant to its actuality.

Those who approach the idea of reincarnation with a mind-set opposed to it, but attuned to popular psychological notions of our time, dismiss the idea as inherently improbable. It is, they say, obviously an example of wish-fulfillment. We are afraid to die, and so we invent a way of getting back into the world. This objection ignores the fact that many of the traditional reincarnationist cultures do not regard rebirth as desirable, but rather as an unfortunate necessity, and their concern is how to escape from the "wheel of birth and death."

Moreover, what is improbable depends on our worldview. Probability is not independent of all our other assumptions about life, but derives from them. To say that reincarnation is improbable tells us nothing about reincarnation, but a good deal about the general assumptions and outlook of the speaker.

Some people also argue that there is no real, solid evidence in support of reincarnation, but they are wrong. The evidence, it is quite true, is inconclusive. It is of a Tweedledee-Tweedledum variety—every kind of evidence in favor can be countered by objections against and alternative explanations. That is so because, finally, reincarnation is not an empirical question.

An empirical question is one that can be answered by experiment and observation. No experiments or observations will finally settle the question of reincarnation one way or the other. It is therefore not an empirical issue, but a metaphysical one. That is, we accept or reject reincarnation, not because a preponderance of evidence can be amassed for or against it, but rather because it fits in or is incompatible with our whole view of the world.

REINCARNATION AS METAPHOR

Reincarnation is metaphorically true. As we pass through the stages of life—child, student, householder and worker, retired person—we develop new personalities to live in the new worlds we inhabit. We die to the old life and are reborn to the next one. And within any one stage of life we also reincarnate. We have one life in our job, a different life in our home, and yet different lives with different sets of friends. And as we go from one of these lives to the next, we "reincarnate." Each night when we go to sleep, we die to the world. Each morning we are reincarnated. Reincarnation is a central part of our experience. Each moment we die and are reincarnated. Consciousness recreates itself ever anew. That means we are not bound to the outworn past. We are not limited to familiar forms and customs, to the ruts of yesterday. By our response to each moment's experience, we reincarnate as a new person. It is painful to be reborn. But it is joyous too. We cannot escape that sort of reincarnation. We can only try to choose our new birth wisely.

Metaphors like reincarnation and life and death are central to the way we see the world and respond to it. Metaphor is a way of coping with reality, perhaps our best way, certainly an indispensable one. Metaphors, or analogies, have always been central to the Wisdom Tradition and a theosophical approach to life. Some people regard the metaphorical truth of reincarnation as an argument against its literal truth—that is, they say it is "just" a metaphor. But to affirm the metaphorical truth of a thing is not to deny it other sorts of truth. Death and birth are metaphors, but they are real enough in themselves.

Belief in reincarnation, metaphorical and literal, is part of belief in a certain kind of world order. It is a metaphysical commitment, with practical consequences. Those who see the world in a reincarnationist way do not require scientific evidence to support their conviction. The evidence is not irrelevant, but it is not—it cannot in the nature of things ever be—conclusive.

Yet evidence there is. And it is to such evidence that we turn in the next four chapters.

5

What Is the Evidence from Mediums?

There is potentially testable evidence of reincarnation from a number of sources: mediumship (today often called channeling), readings by clairvoyants, hypnotic regression, and the spontaneous recall of past lives. Not all of these are equally useful or reliable, and all of them have been challenged. Some are strongly convincing to the persons involved with them, but their evidence may not hold up well under intense public scrutiny. However, if we take all four types of evidence together, collectively they point to something that is hard to ignore. The evidence is not enough to "prove" reincarnation, but it is strongly suggestive of it. The evidence is circumstantial, but the circumstances are remarkable.

In looking at these four sources, it is well to keep in mind something that is often misunderstood and that our language tricks us into misunderstanding. We talk about "proving" something, but strictly speaking nothing can ever be proven, not even a scientific "law." When we say that a scientific principle or law has been "proven," we are saying that (1) the principle explains something for us, (2) we have done our best to find facts that contradict it and have discovered none—at least, no serious ones, and (3) we know of no more satisfactory principle that is similarly free of contradictory facts.

It also helps if the principle is as simple as possible and fits in nicely with other principles that are similarly "proven." In fact, when we say we have "proven" something, we really mean that we have failed to disprove it, despite our best efforts to do just that.

With the foregoing caution in mind, let us look at the four sources of "proof" for reincarnation to see how resistant they are to disproof. The last three, which all involve some form of memory by living persons, will be considered in more detail in the next three chapters, which deal with the evidence of memory.

MEDIUMSHIP AND THE SOCIETY FOR PSYCHICAL RESEARCH

Communications from the dead through mediums might seem to be the very best sort of proof. After all, who should know more about the afterlife than someone who is already there and can speak from direct knowledge? Mediumistic phenomena, however, are very difficult to evaluate. The British Society for Psychical Research and other such bodies have spent a great deal of time and effort in trying to determine the reality and reliability of mediumistic communications. Evaluating such phenomena is a job for those with extensive experience and an impartial eye.

The Society for Psychical Research, founded in 1882, has as its aim "to examine without prejudice or prepossession and in a scientific spirit those faculties of man, real or supposed, which appear to be inexplicable in terms of any generally recognized hypotheses." That aim is fully consonant with the third object of the Theosophical Society, which is "to investigate unexplained laws of nature and the powers latent in man." The two organizations differ in that, whereas the SPR exists solely for the impartial examination of evidence, the Theosoph-

ical Society exists to propound a particular worldview
with implications concerning natural laws and human
faculties.

The Society for Psychical Research was not, however,
entirely impartial in its foundation. Such early members
as Henry Sidgwick, W. F. Barrett, and F. W. H. Myers
found themselves at a time in history when literalist
Christianity was being overthrown by scientific mechanism. Being comfortable with neither of those alter-
natives, they looked to the phenomena of Spiritualism,
which was enjoying a vogue throughout Europe and
America, as possibly offering evidence for the existence
of a nonphysical and nonmechanistic reality. They
hoped that by establishing the reality of such phenomena
(whatever the immediate cause), they would have an
alternative to dead religion and dead science. That same
conflict between religion and science was also a strong
motive force in the foundation of the Theosophical Society, which looked, however, less to Spiritualism than
to the ancient Wisdom Tradition for a middle way.

During the century of its existence, the Society for
Psychical Research has numbered among its presidents
such eminent persons as A. J. Balfour, Prime Minister
of Great Britain from 1902 to 1905; William James, the
American philosopher and psychologist; Sir William
Crookes, a distinguished chemist and physicist; Sir Oliver
Lodge, another distinguished scientist, in physics and
mathematics; Andrew Lang, the anthropologist and
folklorist; Henri Bergson, the French philosopher;
Gilbert Murray, the classicist; Camille Flammarion, the
French astronomer; and J. B. Rhine, the American
parapsychologist. Several of those persons, notably
Crookes and Flammarion, were also members of the
Theosophical Society. The Society for Psychical Research
has studied a variety of paranormal phenomena, always
attempting to approach its subjects with the most rig-

orous methods that can be applied to them. A significant part of those phenomena has involved mediumship.

GARDEN-VARIETY MEDIUMS AND THE WHITE CROW

Some mediums have certainly been frauds (as have
some doctors and lawyers), but most mediums seem to
be quite sincere. Some of the phenomena they produce
are clearly paranormal—since present-day science has
no explanation for those phenomena, and they seem to
violate our everyday assumptions about the world. But
although the phenomena may be genuine, it does not
follow that the Spiritualist explanation is correct. Messages given by a medium are not necessarily from de-
parted spirits. And even if such messages were from a
dead personality, it does not follow that death has con-
ferred upon the late lamented one a sudden insight into
the nature of things.

Most messages purporting to come from discarnate
human beings are platitudinous generalities, and the
process of delivering them, while not deliberate fraud,
is often humbuggery. The medium and the bereaved
have entered into an unstated contract to provide mutual
support. They are both likely to be sincere in what they
are doing.

In a typical "message meeting," the medium is not
in deep, or even light trance. Rather he, or more often
she, senses the presence of a spirit and picks up a name
or a term. The medium will say, "I have a message here
from John. Does 'John' mean anything to anyone here?"
When someone in the group responds, they are likely
to supply additional information, for example, "Oh, that
must be my uncle who passed over last year!" The medium continues, "Well, he wants you to know that he
is happy and loves you. But he used to be rather difficult at times, didn't he." Most people are rather difficult

at times, so the response comes, "He certainly was—he was very fussy about his car especially." "Yes, I could tell that. He was fussy about his car. He didn't like other people to drive it, did he?" And so the exchange goes— the medium building on the responses given by the person for whom the message is supposedly given.

That garden variety of mediumship may comfort the bereaved or the insecure, but it offers no interesting evidence for anything else. It was not the sort investigated by the Society for Psychical Research. They have dealt with much more interesting cases. One of their most famous and impressive mediums was Mrs. Piper from Boston, who was referred to the SPR by William James. She was studied in both America and England by the best minds of the SPR, who found that in her trances she produced "startlingly accurate information" (Haynes 81).

In one session, Mrs. Piper brought through the voice of Katherine, the young daughter of the Rev. Mr. and Mrs. S. W. Sutton. She had died just six weeks before the sitting, and during it spoke of events relating to her death, identified objects she had played with, sang two songs—the only songs she knew in their entirety—used her childish pet names for relatives and dolls, and so on (Rogo *Life* 31). Telepathy was considered as a possibility but ruled out as improbable. Finally, Richard Hodgson, perhaps the most skeptical of all the SPR investigators, concluded that her mediumship "yielded solid evidence for survival and communication" (Haynes 82).

Of Mrs. Piper, William James wrote, "If you wish to upset the law that all crows are black, you must not seek to show that no crows are, it is enough if you prove the single crow to be white. My own white crow is Mrs Piper. In the trances of this medium I cannot resist the conviction that knowledge appears which she has never gained by the ordinary waking use of her eyes and ears and wits." James had no explanation to offer for Mrs. Piper's remarkable abilities. Something paranormal was strongly indicated.

MEDIUM GUIDES AND SECONDARY PERSONALITIES

One possible explanation for the spirit controls or "guides" that most trance mediums use is that they are secondary personalities—bits of the psychic stuff making up our interior life that have gotten dissociated from the primary personality and set up a life of their own. Since we are not simply "souls" occupying bodies, but rather complexes of psychic principles, it is not surprising that those principles can be organized variously within a single person to produce different personalities. These subordinate personalities push their way into expression during states of altered consciousness, as in trances.

Support for such an interpretation came from a series of experiments done during the 1940s and 1950s, involving word-association tests. Tests of that kind have long been used in assessing the psychological state of a subject, who listens to a list of words read aloud and responds to each word with the first thing that comes to mind. The subject's actual response is not at issue— rather what is measured is the time taken to give the response. The theory is that we will reply more slowly to words that affect us emotionally than to others. Each person has a unique set of emotional associations, and so each has a characteristic profile of response times to a given list of words.

The word-association test was given to mediums in their normal consciousness and also when they were in trance, controlled by their guides. The resulting pattern was that words for which the medium's conscious response was slow had a fast response from the trance

guide, and vice versa. The medium's conscious personality and the trance personality were complementary. The
implication is that the trance guide is a part of the
medium's psyche normally active only in the unconscious
state and representing, as unconscious identities often
do, an antithesis to the conscious personality.

However, even if trance guides are really parts of the
medium's psyche, the information that comes through
some mediums, such as Mrs. Piper, cannot be explained
as simply unconscious knowledge. One of the most
famous, long-running, and inexplicable cases of the
Society for Psychical Research is that of the Cross Correspondences.

THE CROSS CORRESPONDENCES

While F. W. H. Myers, one of the founders of the
SPR, was alive, he suggested that good evidence for survival would be a message sent through a number of different mediums who were unaware of one another's
existence, provided each received only part of the total
message. Toward the end of his life, Myers seems to have
tried to analyze the productions of several mediums in
that way, but without success. Shortly after his death
in 1901, however, messages began to come by automatic
writing, produced at the same times but on different
continents by mediums completely ignorant of one
another. Some messages stated the same ideas in different
words. Others were meaningless alone, but made sense
only when combined with those from other sources.

The "Cross Correspondences," as such messages were
known, continued for a period of some years, frequently
seeming to be of a complexity matched only by the intricacies of the crossword puzzle in the London *Times*,
"with its anagrams, its quotations, its cryptic allusions
to a vast variety of subjects: classics, current events, phi-

losophy, proverbs, old songs, sport" (Haynes 71). The Cross Correspondences, which include about 3000 scripts, were thus a very English phenomenon. Some of them include such personal material that they are under seal at Trinity College, Cambridge, not to be made available for general study until the year 2000, by which time the participants and their children will all be deceased.

One Cross Correspondence is the Palm Sunday case. In it, messages were received by a number of mediums who knew nothing whatever about the facts to which the messages alluded. They involved the love of Arthur Balfour, when he was a young man, for Mary Catherine Lyttelton. She died of typhoid fever on Palm Sunday, 1875, and was buried with his mother's emerald ring on her finger. He kept a lock of her golden brown hair in a silver box he had made for it. He never married. The messages alluded to his name and Mary's, to the ring, the hair, the box, the date of her death, and so on (Haynes 72).

Another Cross Correspondence was that of the Medici Tombs. The messages contained allusions to dawn, evening and morning, death, laurel, shadows, sleep, the apparent name *Morehead,* a Negro, and Alexander's tomb. Eventually, one medium produced the message "Laurential tomb, Dawn and Twilight," which proved to be the key to the case. The messages concerned the tombs of the Medici family. The laurel was the emblem of Lorenzo de Medici, patriarch of the family. The tombs are carved with allegorical representations of dawn and twilight. Alessandro de Medici, who had been secretly buried in the tombs, was nicknamed "the Moor" because he was part black in ancestry (Rogo *Life* 35-37).

The intricacies of the Cross Correspondence puzzles are hard to explain in any except some paranormal way. Perhaps a disembodied Myers was playing literary and historical games of a sort he had, while alive, proposed as a convincing proof of survival. Perhaps they are instances of an elaborate Jungian synchronicity—the coincidence of meaningfully related but causally unconnected facts. In any case, they have no rational explanation of a materialistic sort.

XENOGLOSSY

A different sort of evidence is that of xenoglossy—the use of a foreign language by one who has never studied or been exposed to it, at least in the present life. Ian Stevenson, a psychiatrist who has meticulously investigated possible memories of past lives, has studied cases of this kind, especially that of a medium, a physician's wife identified only as T.E. During a series of hypnotic experiments conducted by her husband, T.E. began to manifest the personality of a Scandinavian peasant farmer named Jensen Jacoby, who apparently had lived near the Norwegian-Swedish border perhaps in the seventeenth century. In that personality, she began to speak snatches of a foreign language eventually identified as an old form of Swedish, with an admixture of Norwegian and Danish elements.

The Jensen personality spoke in and responded to both English and Swedish or Norwegian (the latter two being very similar languages). Once T.E.'s husband realized the unusualness of the xenoglossic performance by his wife, the sessions were tape recorded, and transcripts of those recordings have been made. Also native speakers of Swedish sat in on all the sessions after the fifth, and engaged the Jensen personality in conversation in Swedish.

Stevenson's investigation of T.E.'s background revealed no acquaintance with any Scandinavian language. Lie detector tests administered to both T.E. and her husband showed them to be honest in their denial of knowledge of any such language. Stevenson concluded that the most likely explanation is that either the surviving spirit of Jensen Jacoby was manifesting through T.E. as medium, or that Jensen was a former incarnation of T.E.'s, whose memories she had resurrected. He was unable to choose between those possibilities on the basis of the evidence.

A linguist, Sarah Grey Thomason, has also investigated some supposed cases of xenoglossy under hypnosis, which were, however, much weaker than that of T.E. Her conclusions were that the supposedly foreign languages—Bulgarian, Gaelic, and Apache—were actually fluent gibberish. The cases she studied would thus seem to have been instances of secular glossolalia, rather than xenoglossy. Glossolalia is the production of a fluent stream of sounds that seem language-like but are no known language and in fact are lacking the sort of grammatical patterns that human languages always show. Glossolalia is widely practiced by some religious groups as a form of the "speaking in tongues" attributed to the Apostles at Pentecost.

Glossolalia and xenoglossy are opposite phenomena. In glossolalia, the hearers are supposed to understand the speech, and in churches where it is practiced, typically some member of the congregation "interprets" the glossolalic utterance for the other members of the congregation. It is not assumed that the language is any normal human tongue. In xenoglossy, a normal human language is supposedly used by one who has never studied it or been exposed to it. If genuine xenoglossy is attested, it is strong evidence for the paranormal. Well attested cases, as opposed to anecdotal ones, however, are very rare—Stevenson's being almost unique.

CONCLUSION

A recently popular form of mediumship known as "channeling" has the same weaknesses as other forms of mediumship. The "discarnate entities" that speak through the medium-channeler in most cases can be explained as dissociated parts of the medium's own psyche that have taken on separate identities and are acting out roles. Some may also be emotional-mental complexes from outside the medium-channeler that have intruded into the medium's awareness. But they are probably seldom, if ever, what they purport to be.

The danger in any form of real mediumship is that the "communicator," whether it be a fragment of the medium's psyche or an outside influence, will take command of the medium's consciousness and thereby produce undesirable consequences. Casual mediumship is hardly more than a parlor game, though it too has its dangerous side.

Spiritualism and mediums have undoubtedly provided comfort and reassurance for many. And really talented mediums like Mrs. Piper have offered puzzles that the most skillful investigators have been unable to solve. Nevertheless, whatever mediumship has shown about the survival of the personality after death, the evidence it provides for reincarnation is weak at best. There are better sources, which involve the memories of living persons. It is to them that we turn in the next three chapters.

6

Can We Remember Subliminally and Clairvoyantly?

A frequent objection to reincarnation is that if we have lived before, we ought to remember. And if we cannot remember, then it is not really we who have lived before, because continuity of consciousness implies continuity of memory. Memory, it is said, is what makes us the "same" person from one time to another.

SUBLIMINAL MEMORY

It can be argued that all of us do remember our past lives —although in ways that we may not recognize. To begin with, there are various kinds of memory. Most of us can remember very little about having learned to drive a car or use a typewriter, but the results of that learning are still very much with us as a subliminal memory, a memory beneath the threshold of consciousness—we drive and type as though no learning had been needed for those activities. We probably cannot remember at all having learned to read or to walk on two legs, and yet we read and walk quite naturally. One kind of memory is for specific events—taking driving lessons or practicing on a typewriter. Another kind is the habitual though unconscious ability to perform a task that originally required conscious learning.

Those different kinds of memory are parallel to different kinds of knowledge. English is very poor in words for mental functions. We use *know* for some quite diverse mental states. We say that we "know" the world is round, that we "know" Chicago, that we "know" chess. But those are three very different forms of knowledge. To know a fact like the roundness of the earth is to realize its truth. To know a city like Chicago is to have been there. To know a game like chess is to be able to play it. Some languages very sensibly use different verbs for those three kinds of knowing, but English lumps them all together.

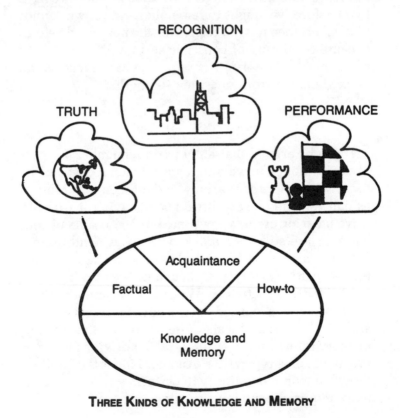

THREE KINDS OF KNOWLEDGE AND MEMORY

To each kind of knowing there is a corresponding kind of remembering. To remember a fact is to be able to repeat it. To remember a place is to recognize it when we encounter it again. To remember a game is to be able to play it after some time has elapsed. We can call those three kinds of memory, respectively, factual memory, acquaintance memory, and how-to memory. And similarly those kinds of memory are based on factual, acquaintance, and how-to knowledge.

How-to knowledge and memory are the most tenacious and the most important of the lot. Almost no one has any acquaintance memory of having learned to speak English, or whatever one's native language may be. The learning happened too long ago, when we were too young to remember much of anything. Now it is completely subliminal. Very few people have ever had much factual knowledge about their native language; those who do are likely to be linguists or grammarians.

For example: *Any* and *some* have approximately the same meaning but are used in quite different ways ("I have some" but not "I have any"). When is each word used? Unless you have studied English linguistics, you are very unlikely to know the answer to that question; yet you consistently use those two words in a regular way. We learn how to speak our native language without ever learning to state the rules that describe what we are doing. To have how-to knowledge and memory, it is not necessary ever to have had factual knowledge.

With regard to reincarnation, these various kinds of memory imply that we may remember our past lives in one way, but not in another. We may not remember facts from previous lifetimes, and we may not remember acquaintances from them, yet we may remember how to do certain things that we learned in past lifetimes.

To be sure, knowing how to use a typewriter in this lifetime does not mean you will be able to type when you come back about the year 2304 (assuming that type-writers are still around then). The memory of how to do things like type and drive a car is located in the nervous system and dies with the body. But an interest in machines and gadgets, a curiosity about how they work, a facility for learning how to operate them—this more abstract and generalized form of knowledge, which is really a propensity for learning rather than a specific accomplishment, may well survive from one incarnation to another. It is likely that Thomas Alva Edison did not start tinkering with things for the first time in his 1847–1931 life but had done it before.

Because our personal memory is very much tied up with our physical body and brain, we should expect that it will disappear when the body and all its organs do. Only the more abstract skills and concepts would normally be expected to carry over from one lifetime to another. And yet there are occasions when other kinds of memories seem to come through, times when genuine personal memories—of persons, places, languages, events, fears, and ambitions—seem to survive. The mechanisms by which personal memories from a past life can be available in this one probably vary according to the circumstances of the recall. In the remainder of this chapter and in the next two, we consider three kinds of exceptional survival of personal memories of a past life, three ways in which memory of past lives can rise above the threshold of consciousness and become superliminal.

CLAIRVOYANT PERCEPTION OF THE PAST

The first kind of past-life memory is not a personal memory, but an impersonal, external one. Some persons have a type of clairvoyance that allows them to do what might be called "tapping into the memory of nature." According to the Wisdom Tradition, nature records all things that have ever occurred, and therefore it is possible to recover information about the past, including past lives of another person. The most famous and remarkable of such sensitives in the twentieth century was Edgar Cayce (1877–1945).

As a child in Kentucky, Cayce had a variety of paranormal experiences: he saw and talked with recently deceased relatives, and he developed a photographic memory. As a young man he developed an acute case of laryngitis, which he cured by entering a trance state in which he diagnosed his own ailment and prescribed a treatment for it.

As a result of Cayce's success in curing himself, he was called upon by medical persons to assist in treating others. Cayce would enter a trance state and then examine the physical body of a patient, who did not need to be present at the time of the examination. Still in the trance, Cayce would analyze the cause of the patient's sickness and suggest remedies. Cayce conducted "physical readings" of this type for about twenty-five years before his clairvoyance took a different tack.

Because Cayce had no recollection of what he had said during a trance, a stenographer wrote down his analysis of each case (and those stenographic records are still in existence, forming the material which is studied by a foundation Cayce left behind him). In 1923, upon reviewing one of the transcriptions, Cayce himself was much surprised by what he had said in trance. In this reading, he talked about reincarnation as an indisputable fact. Cayce was an orthodox member of a Protestant church and a Sunday school teacher who read the Bible through each year and accepted a generally literalist interpretation of it. Reincarnation seemed to be a bizarre notion.

Cayce, however, continued with his trance investiga-

tions, which were increasingly directed toward analyz-
ing the causes of present illness in terms of past-life
experiences. Those sessions that focused on reincarnation and the earlier lives of the subjects are known as
"life readings." There are approximately 2500 of them.

However, there is a problem with information about
past lives as reported by sensitives, even such a talented
one as Cayce. The former personality of the client would
have been either obscure or prominent. If the past life
identity was obscure, it is very difficult to check the accuracy of facts reported about it, however detailed and
specific they may be. Records of ordinary people were
poorly kept in the past.

If, on the other hand, the former incarnation was as
a famous person, then the facts of that person's life will
be described in books and so might have been known
to the sensitive by normal means. The "readings" of a
sensitive about past lives are almost always subject to
this Catch-22. It is extremely rare that the information
can be checked for accuracy in a source that probably
could not have been available to the sensitive. Therefore,
most past-life readings are not helpful as evidence about
reincarnation, however useful they may be for other
purposes.

Because Cayce's life readings are usually not detailed
and specific enough to allow historical checks on their
accuracy they do not provide convincing scientific
evidence of reincarnation. But the remarkable thing
about them is the accuracy of their delineation of the
character of the subjects. Efforts have been made by
Cayce's foundation to trace the subsequent history of
the persons for whom he gave readings, to see whether
their lives followed the patterns described by Cayce and
whether his analysis proved helpful. An impressive
number of the subjects believe that Cayce's readings
were accurate and that his recommendations were
sound.

How can such insight into character and such apparent knowledge of the past lives of others be explained? How can one person "remember" the past of another? The nature of memory is poorly understood. It is usually thought of as a matter of storage, somehow, of traces of past experience in the cells of the brain. Certainly the brain plays an important role in memory, but no one has ever been able to propose an explanation of memory that is convincing and is also purely physicalist (one that accounts for it solely as a matter of electrical or chemical activity in brain cells). The truth is that we do not know exactly how ordinary memory works, much less the extraordinary sort of memory that Cayce seemed to have.

THE AKASHIC RECORDS AND MEMORY

One theory of memory within the Wisdom Tradition does, however, provide an explanation for what Cayce and other such investigators have been able to do. It is called "reading the akashic records" or "viewing the astral light." (*Akasha* is a term from Hindu philosophy for a kind of subtle, plastic substance that can be impressed with a record of events; *astral light* is a corresponding nineteenth-century European term.)

The "akashic records" have been called the memory of nature, the record of everything that has been thought or felt or done since the beginning of time. As such, they might be thought of as the subconscious mind of the whole human race, or even of life itself. Thus the akashic records can be compared to the Jungian concept of the collective unconscious.

Another way of thinking about the akashic records is to regard them simply as a matter of perceiving dimensions of reality more fully than we normally do. The space in which we live has three dimensions. Mathematicians, theoretical physicists, and mystics sometimes postulate more spatial dimensions—a fourth or fifth or even

greater numbers. But three dimensions of space are all
we know. However, we do experience, in a restricted
way, a fourth dimension—time.

Clearly, things persist in time. They have chronological continuity, although their forms change with time.
Your body today has developed out of what it was ten
years ago and will change into something different in
the future. Your whole physical body is all the shapes
it has been in the past and all those it will be in the
future, not just the form it happens to be in at the present moment. Your total body transcends the limitations
of time because it extends through time into the past and
the future.

We are normally aware of only the present moment,
although that moment is constantly changing, flowing
into what was the future and leaving behind what used
to be the present but has become the past. Time is a dimension of which we have sharply limited awareness.
Our focus is our perception of the present. Otherwise
we normally have only a memory of the past and an an-
ticipation of the future. But things exist along the dimension of time, as well as along spatial dimensions.

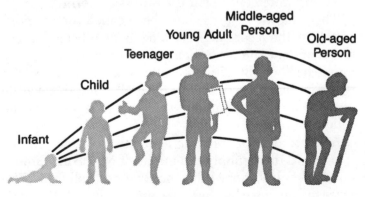

THE BODY IN TIME

Think of time as a straight line. Each moment is a point on the line. Just as the line contains an infinite number of points, because they have no dimension whatever, so time contains an infinite number of moments, which have no duration. Now imagine that you cannot see the line as a whole, but that your vision is forced to travel along the line in one direction only, constantly moving so that it passes over one point on the line after another. Points that you have not yet come to would be the future for you. Points that you had already gone by would be a memory from the past. Only the dimensionless point you were focusing on would seem to exist—it would be your present. In such restricted conditions, the line would be only a theoretical reality; all that would actually exist in your awareness would be the point of momentary focus. That is the way we perceive time normally—with just such severe restrictions.

Now imagine that you are suddenly able to pull back, into another dimension, and see the whole line with beginning, end, and extension in between. That, of course, is the way we in fact see lines. Now you perceive the line as a unit, whereas before you saw only arbitrarily restricted parts of it. If we could similarly draw back into some other dimension of reality (a dimension called "eternity") outside of time, then we could see the whole form of things, with beginning, development, and end, whereas now we see things only moment by moment, never wholly.

Of Edgar Cayce's ability to look into the past and the future, we can say (as he did) that he was reading the akashic records. And by that we can understand that he had tapped into the memory of nature, the collective unconscious of the life force. Or we can also say that he had backed a little way out of time and so was able to look at larger parts of the line of the reincarnating lives of those who came to him for "readings." Cayce was not "remembering" anything personally; he was looking directly at a part of reality that most of us do not normally see.

GROUP REINCARNATION

Cayce is not the only clairvoyant thus to "read" the akashic records. Others have done so as well, and an interesting conclusion can be drawn from such studies. It appears from them that the incarnations of an individual are not random with respect to other individuals. Rather than being born among a new group each lifetime, we tend to be reborn with the same individuals.

It would appear that souls cluster into reincarnational communities, which tend to come into life together. A little thought will show that this effect is not at all surprising, but is instead exactly what we might predict according to the principle of karma. In any given lifetime, we contract karmic debts with those about us. The debts may be of love or hatred, of friendship or suspicion, of cooperation or shared guilt, of patronage or servitude—the nature of the tie is less important than the fact that we have, for whatever reason, bonded ourselves with others.

Those bonds will serve to draw us and persons with whom we are bound into incarnation at the same time and place, so the bonds can be worked out. But typically in trying to work out old bonds, we form new ones with the same persons, which must in turn be worked out in a later life. And thus come into existence these loose groups that may be called reincarnational communities, in which most of the members have karmic ties with other members.

One of the best known recent accounts of group reincarnation is that recorded by Arthur Guirdham, a

British psychiatrist. In the course of treating a woman suffering from recurrent nightmares, his own memories of a former incarnation as a Cathar priest among the Albigensians of thirteenth-century France were activated. He recalled that he, his patient, and (as eventually appeared) a number of other persons known to them in this life had lived together before, not only in the Albigensian community but also in several other settings. Because Guirdham has refused on grounds of medical confidentiality to reveal the present identities of his patient and others in the reincarnational group, his account is unconfirmed.

Such a succession of mutually related incarnations of the same group of persons has seemed to some to be inherently implausible. But, if reincarnation and karma are facts, there is nothing implausible about it. In that case, the chances are very good that many of the persons associated with us in any given lifetime are reincarnations of persons we have been associated with before. We may not remember, in a simple sense, those with whom we have formed bonds in past lives, but our ties with them lead to a kind of recognition. We know them subliminally. They are old acquaintances.

7

Can We Remember Hypnotically?

Of the forms of past-life memory considered in the last chapter, subliminal memory is common to all of us and clairvoyant perception is limited to a very few in whom it has developed exceptionally. The two forms of memory taken up in this chapter and in the next are to be found in ordinary persons without special training. One is deliberately induced, the other is a spontaneous event.

HYPNOSIS AS THERAPY

The deliberately induced type of memory is one in which an individual appears to recall his or her own past lives, with the aid of an artificial stimulus—hypnotic suggestion. A basic technique of modern psychotherapy is to have patients recall forgotten events from earlier life. The assumption is that many dysfunctions in the present—psychological problems, neuroses, mentally caused illnesses—are the result of painful experiences in the past which we have deliberately forgotten or repressed. To cure these psychological illnesses, the cause must be treated, not just the symptoms. Therefore it is necessary for those with such an illness to realize its cause, in order to come to terms with that part of their lives that they have repressed. Hence the psychiatrist's couch and the technique of letting patients talk out their problems.

Frequently, however, such patients have difficulty in bringing painful memories into consciousness. So a number of techniques have been developed to assist recall. One is dream analysis; in dreams, a patient may symbolically express ideas or memories that are too frightening to face directly in conscious awareness. Hypnosis can also be used to improve memory, even of quite ordinary matters. For example, if someone has hidden away an object for safekeeping and then forgotten where it is, hypnosis may help to find it. Through the assistance of this technique, things once known, even quite casually, and then long forgotten can be brought back into awareness with a fullness, detail, and accuracy that is amazing. So some psychotherapists started using hypnosis to help their patients with the process of therapeutic recall.

Some psychologists believe that warps in the personality of an adult are sometimes caused by experiences in earliest infancy or even by the trauma of birth—leaving the warm, dark security of the womb for the cold, piercingly bright uncertainty of independent existence as a person. Some have gone so far as to suppose that prenatal experiences—trauma in the womb—may be the cause of psychic malfunction in later life. Those events would be completely out of reach for the consciously controllable memory, so it was natural for psychotherapists to try hypnosis as a device to help recall them.

Going back in time imaginatively under hypnosis to recover forgotten memories is called *regression*. As psychotherapists regressed their patients further and further back—to infancy, the birth experience, and prenatal existence—some patients were pushed back into memories they reported to be of prior incarnations. And so hypnotic regression became a widely used tool for investigating past lives.

THE CASE OF BRIDEY MURPHY

Investigations of past lives by hypnosis (or mesmerism, as it was called earlier) had been made since the second half of the nineteenth century, but the technique has come to be widely used only since the late 1950s. The most famous case about that time was that of a Colorado housewife who was regressed by a hypnotist, Morey Bernstein, expressly in an effort to establish evidence for reincarnation. Under hypnosis, the subject remembered her life in the early nineteenth century as a lower-middle-class Irish woman. The case was described in a book called *The Search for Bridey Murphy*.

Bridey had lived in Cork and Belfast and married Brian MacCarthy, a barrister. She had traded with a grocer named John Carrigan and with another named Farr. Her husband, who was Catholic whereas she was Protestant, attended St. Theresa's Church and wrote for a Belfast newspaper, the *Newsletter*. Details of this sort can be verified, and a number of those given about Bridey did indeed check out. Others are unconfirmed, but possible.

The case of Bridey Murphy and the book about her became famous, if not infamous. Some church ministers, who were anxious about the implications of reincarnational memories for their own views of reality, came into league with several magazines and newspapers that were glad to debunk the case for the boost the publicity would give their circulations.

Charges were made that the hypnotized subject had an Irish aunt from whom she had heard stories about Ireland as a child and that she had also had a neighbor called "Bridey Murphy." However, the aunt turned out to know very little about Ireland (like most Irish Americans) and to have had no contact with her niece as a child. There was a neighbor named "Bridey," but that is a common Irish name (short for "Bridget"), and the neighbor's last name was not "Murphy," but she was the mother of the editor who made the false charges.

The resulting controversy was so confused that it is impossible today to judge the reliability of the Bridey Murphy case. It may have been an example of cryptomnesia ("hidden memory"), a phenomenon by which we learn things in a normal way but then forget the source of our learning, so that the knowledge appears to come from a mysterious source. Or it may have included some genuine memories of a past life. But it certainly focused attention on reincarnation and led to the increased use of past-life hypnotic regression.

UNCONSCIOUS PLAYACTING AND FAR MEMORY

The question of the nature of hypnotic regression is an open one. Are the experiences genuine memories of past lives, or something else? The most likely alternative is that they are dramatized communications from the subject's own subconscious, mixed with information learned casually and forgotten by the conscious mind. In a state of hypnosis, when the subconscious is more available than normally, there is a strong desire to please —to do what is wanted. So if the subconscious receives a directive to recount a past life, that is exactly what it does. And it does so by inventing a plausible scenario out of whatever knowledge it has of the period in question.

It is likely that many, if not most, apparent cases of past-life regression under hypnosis, especially the light sort of hypnosis that is often used, are play-acting by the unconscious. Such play-acting may, however, have a serious purpose and a beneficial effect. The sub-conscious may take the opportunity of dramatizing to express itself about any psychological problems the subject is experiencing. If the past-life regression is done in a therapeutic setting, it is especially likely that the dramatization, whether it reports the facts of a past life or is an imaginative projection of the causes of a present problem, will have therapeutic implications.

At the same time, it is possible and in some cases likely that real past-life memories are brought through at least occasionally in past-life regressions. Even when accurate, however, such apparent memories are not memories in the usual sense. A twentieth-century brain can hardly remember events that affected a seventeenth-century or a third-century-B.C. brain, long since returned to its elements.

Perhaps what happens in hypnotic regression is similar to Edgar Cayce's reading of the akashic records. A hypnotized subject may be sufficiently distanced from the physical limitations of the body that he or she is able to tap into the memory of nature—to look down on the time dimension—or at least that portion of it relating most closely to his or her own past incarnations. It is impossible to say how often such genuine perception of the past occurs because most accounts of past lives through hypnotic regression are too unspecific to make rigorous checking feasible. The best that can be said for most of them is that they are suggestive of a real report.

REGRESSIONS IN BREADTH AND DEPTH

An active experimenter in hypnotic regression is the psychologist Helen Wambach. Over a period of ten years, she conducted approximately 2000 regression sessions. She developed a technique by which she regressed groups of persons at the same time and through post-hypnotic suggestion enlisted their aid in remembering and recording their hypnotic past-life impressions. The result was an unusually broad survey.

One of the noteworthy features of her cases is that the subjects do not usually create for themselves interesting or ego-stroking past lives, as they might be expected to do if their unconscious minds were inventing a fantasy. When we fantasize roles for ourselves in our daydreams, we are usually important, accomplished figures who are the center of attention. However, typical of the memories of Wambach's subjects were a retarded shepherd who was happy to be surrounded by his sheep and a New Guinea native, terrified by the taboos of her tribe, whose life was poor, nasty, brutish, and short. Hardly the stuff daydreams are made of.

It is also significant that statistically Wambach's many sessions of regression have a reasonable demographic spread. For example, about 60 to 75 percent of the remembered lives were lower class socially, 20 to 35 percent were middle class, and on average only about 5 percent were upper class. That is not an improbable distribution for most periods of human history.

The statistics about sex were equally interesting. Surveys of the population have shown that, given their choice, the average person would prefer to be a man rather than a woman—a fact probably reflecting the greater social and biological freedom men typically have. If the apparent memories were really fantasies, one would expect a preponderance of male past lives. But in fact, in two sizable groups, slightly more than 50 percent of the past lives were as males and slightly less than 50 percent were as females (50.3 versus 49.7 and 50.9 versus 49.1). Furthermore, this approximately even distribution was not affected by the makeup of the groups, one of which had a preponderance of women and the other a more even balance of women and men.

The Wambach regressions are suggestive, especially in the aggregate. But the individual cases are too general and verifying the facts reported would be too difficult for these cases to be convincing evidence of reincarnation. An in-depth study of a single subject of regression was made by Jonathan Venn. He conducted sixty hypnotic interviews with the same subject, made extensive efforts to confirm or disconfirm all facts reported, and weighed reincarnation against other possible explanations of the purported memories.

Venn's subject was Matthew, a twenty-six-year-old optometrist's assistant who hypnotically relived an earlier life as a French aviator, Jacques Gionne Trecaultes, shot down by a German plane over Belgium in 1914. The French that he occasionally used was poor and obviously that of a foreigner, according to a native speaker who evaluated it. However, under hypnosis Matthew had an impressive store of information about World War I, the technical details of early military aviation, and the geography of France. He also made about twice as many factual errors as correct statements in his descriptions.

Venn compared the truth or falsehood of the statements the hypnotized Matthew made with the ease or difficulty of acquiring the information. He concluded that Matthew's "hits" were all the sort of information that is commonly available, whereas his "misses" were about evenly divided between facts commonly available and those available only in recondite sources. It seems likely, then, that Matthew's subconscious invented the personality of the French pilot and fleshed it out with accurate information acquired from popular sources and with imaginary, unfactual details.

Venn's carefully studied case provides no evidence for reincarnation, only for cryptomnesia and subconscious dramatization. However, it is only a single case and does not preclude the possibility of other regressions being genuine examples of past-life memories.

THE BLOXHAM TAPES

More arresting examples of apparent past-life memories are in the Bloxham tapes. They are taped records of some 400 regressions conducted by Arnell Bloxham, president of the British Society of Hypnotherapists. A BBC television program based on the tapes created a sensation in the United Kingdom when it was shown in 1976. Efforts have been made to verify details from the Bloxham tapes, and with some striking successes.

One remarkable case involved the regression of a Welsh housewife, given the pseudonym of "Jane Evans," to six earlier lives:

1. Livonia, the wife of Titus, a tutor to the son of the governor of Roman Britain. This incarnation took place in the late third century, the governor being Constantius, his wife Helena, and his son Constantine, who was later to become the first Christian emperor of Rome. An interesting aspect of this memory is that Constantius is not known ever to have been governor of Britain, but the years of his life between 283 and 290 are unaccounted for, the identity of the Roman governor of Britain at that period is unknown, and those years are the focus of the "Livonia" memories. A large number of the other memories of "Livonia" about events, people, and places are correct.

2. Rebecca, a Jewess living in England in the late twelfth century and killed during the York Massacre of 1190. "Rebecca" recounted that, during a mob uprising against the Jews, her family was refused admission to the castle (where in fact most of the Jews of the town

were sheltered against the mob). Instead, she and her family took refuge in the crypt of a small church outside "the big copper gate of York."

The detail of the place of refuge is important because, if the hypnotic account had been based on a remembered historical account of the persecution, Jane Evans would have been likely to choose the castle for refuge, that being where most of the Jews fled (only to be betrayed and murdered later). The castle figures prominently in historical reports, whereas no church does.

Even more significant is the fact that the church "Rebecca" described is almost surely St. Mary's, Castlegate. Yet neither it nor any of the forty other churches of York was known to have a crypt. Only the cathedral had one, and "Rebecca" specifically denied having taken refuge in it. The account appeared to be wrong. However, during a later remodeling of the church, evidence of a crypt beneath its chancel was discovered, thus confirming this highly improbable detail, about which the hypnotized subject could not possibly have known.

The dramatic conviction with which Jane Evans told the story of her "Rebecca" personality also impressed many who heard it. In describing her fruitless efforts to escape the mob and protect her daughter by hiding in the crypt, she became hysterical with terror. On leaving the session, Jane Evans fainted and was frightened and ill for days afterwards. If some of the Bloxham tapes are not what they purport to be—the relived memories of episodes from past lives—they are just as great mysteries of another kind.

3. Alison, an Egyptian servant brought to France by Jacques Coeur, a wealthy merchant and financial advisor to King Charles VII. For this life Jane Evans remembered a wealth of specific details about Jacques Coeur's life and dealings with the French court, many

of which were subsequently confirmed. An interesting minor detail is that "Alison" described a golden apple as a prize possession of Coeur's, which he kept in his treasury. Although no such object was known, a symbolic carving over the door of his castle depicted an orange tree, and the French for orange is *pomme d'or,* literally 'apple of gold.' Eventually, intense research uncovered a record of objects confiscated from Coeur after his eventual disgrace, and among them was a golden pomegranate, a fruit whose name means 'apple full of seeds.'

4. Anna, a servant to Catherine of Aragon, who traveled with her mistress to England in 1501, when Catherine was to wed Prince Arthur, the eldest son of Henry VII. Anna, about seventeen at the time, was rebellious against the puritanical customs of the pious Spanish court. She was sent back to Spain shortly after the wedding.

5. Ann Tasker, a poor, uneducated London girl who worked for a seamstress during the reign of Queen Anne. In this personality, Jane Evans was uncommunicative, bordering on the surly. She seemed ill-informed about life around her and resentful of questioning.

6. Sister Grace, a nun from Des Moines, Iowa, who lived approximately 1860 to 1920. She was apparently a member of the order of the Sisters of Mercy in Maryland. She worked in the kitchen, being a simple soul with a mischievous sense of humor and no strong inclination for the religious life. Consequently, she had wistful regrets about missing life in the outside world, which she never knew.

It is noteworthy that these six earlier incarnations were all strikingly different in personality from each other and from the present-day Jane Evans. Such contrast of personality is to be seen also in several other of the Bloxham regressions, such as that of Graham Huxtable, a refined citizen of Swansea who relived a life as a crude but vigorous young farmer lad who was impressed for service as a gunner's mate on a British frigate he called "the *Aggie*" during England's eighteenth-century wars with France.

The detail and authenticity of Huxtable's descriptions of seafaring, with which he had no familiarity in his present life, and the dramatic realism of his account of being wounded in a battle off Calais captured the attention of the late Earl Mountbatten and of Prince Philip. They tried with the aid of naval historians to identify the battle. However, the long drawn-out war against France with its multitude of skirmishes is too poorly documented to link the seaman's wounding and probable death with any specific battle.

EVALUATING HYPNOTIC REGRESSION

As therapy, past-life regression seems often to be successful. Many of those who have experienced it either as therapist or as patient are enthusiastic about its results. Nevertheless, hypnosis has its dangers. One is that it may produce a variety of unpleasant side effects, such as headaches and feelings of anxiety. Another is that in hypnotic regression the past-life personality sometimes begins to monopolize the consciousness of the patient, so that psychological and even physical characteristics of that personality intrude on the present life. Thus instead of promoting the integration of the personality, hypnosis may lead to its fragmentation. Another danger is that the patient will begin to substitute the excitement of discovering past lives for the tedium of coping with problems in the present life. That is, regression therapy can become just another device for avoiding reality. Sometimes, like any other therapy, it simply does not work—there is no result.

In general, the theosophical tradition discourages casual use of any technique—such as hypnotism, drug-taking, or mediumship—in which the conscious mind is artificially bypassed and the subconscious is made into a passive receiver of influences from whatever source. We do not improve our grasp of reality by anesthetizing the mind.

However salutary or dangerous past-life regression may be as psychological therapy, as evidence of reincarnation it is typically no more useful than the readings of sensitives. The reasons are the same: either the facts about the past life are too obscure to verify, or they are so well known that they could have been learned in ordinary ways.

In addition, the propensity of the subconscious mind to dramatize, to play roles, and its amenability to suggestion under hypnosis confuse the question of what the memories really are. If the therapist asks a hypnotized patient to go back to some earlier life, the subconscious mind duly obliges by making up a story about what such an earlier life might have been like. In the process of dramatization, the subconscious may well work out some problem that has been debilitating the patient and thus restore psychological health. But the fact that past-life regression is sometimes effective therapy is not a guarantee that it is true.

Although hypnotically induced memory does not provide firm evidence for reincarnation, it is a phenomenon to be reckoned with. Some "memories" from hypnosis are almost certainly dramatizations by the subconscious, but others cannot easily be explained in that way. For those others, there is no better explanation than that they are exactly what they seem to be—memories, subject to the distortion of all memory, of events that happened long ago and far away, events from other lifetimes.

8

Can We Remember Spontaneously?

*P*erhaps the most impressive memories of past lives are not summoned up by a psychic or induced by hypnosis, but occur spontaneously. Spontaneous memories are of two kinds: those in adults, which are mainly sporadic impressions of a particular scene, and those in young children, which are of various persons, things, and events. Adult memories are like hypnotically induced ones in that they often involve reliving a scene. Childhood memories are more like our normal recollection of the past.

ADULT MEMORIES

Frederick Lenz has studied the spontaneous appearance in adults of memories apparently from past lives. These memories appear suddenly, are extremely vivid, and endure in that vivid state for only a few minutes. The experience has something in common with, and may be preceded by, an experience of déjà vu. The memory may be triggered by meeting a person, hearing a piece of music, or seeing an object. Sometimes the memory comes during ordinary waking life, sometimes during a dream of extraordinary vividness, and sometimes during prayer or meditation. In every case, a special or "altered" state of consciousness seems to be involved. The onset of the memory may be heralded by a high-pitched, ringing sound of increasing intensity, a sensation of floating, a haziness of vision with colored lights, a perception of vibration in the surroundings, a feeling of separation from the physical body, the impression of moving through a tunnel with a bright light at the end, or a sense of euphoria—of profound well-being. The memory may begin with a movie-like rapid review of the events of the past life, before the subject enters into the "movie" and becomes part of it. There may be a voice or "guide" who comments on the events of the life and assists with forming a judgment of it. Some of these features also appear in near-death experiences (discussed in chapter 10) and so are probably associated with a disentanglement from one's present personal life.

After the onset experiences, the person finds himself or herself in a different time and place, reliving what seems to be a moment out of a past life. Another investigator, D. Scott Rogo, examined a smaller number of cases than Lenz, but did so more carefully. He found similar examples of spontaneous past-life recall, although without the onset phenomena of sounds and other sensations that Lenz thought typical of the phenomenon.

As mentioned above, these spontaneous memories of a past life also have some similarity to those induced by hypnotic regression. Indeed, the memories themselves seem to be essentially the same sort of experience, only with different methods of producing them. The apparently altered state of consciousness associated with the sudden appearance of spontaneous memories is like a hypnotic state that has been accidentally induced.

A different sort of adult memory is that reported by Edward W. Ryall in his book *Born Twice: Total Recall of a Seventeenth-century Life*. Ryall, born in 1902, claims recollections from early childhood of a previous life as John Fletcher (1645-85), a farmer in Somerset who was killed while serving as a scout at the Battle of Sedgemoor in the Monmouth Rebellion.

The case is unusual in that Ryall's recollections appear to have increased during his lifetime, instead of fading as is normal with childhood memories. Also they include a very large number of specific details covering the whole of the remembered life, instead of only one or two scenes, as is typical of most adult memories of former lives.

Part of the weakness of Ryall's case as evidence for reincarnation is that he did not reveal his memories to any of his contemporaries until he was of mature years. In 1970, Ryall answered an ad in the *Daily Express*, calling for readers to send accounts of memories of past lives to the paper. He claims to have talked of such memories when he was a child, but his father and other older family members to whom he told them are now dead. Consequently, no independent witness of Ryall's early memories now exists.

Some of the specific details Ryall relates have been confirmed as factual, but there are also some errors and anachronisms. The sexual scenarios remembered by Ryall are both melodramatic and mildly sensational; they are also improbable for the time and place. The tone of the part of the book treating his marital arrangements is reminiscent of a rather ordinary historical novel.

There is no reason to believe that Ryall was perpetrating a hoax, but neither is there much reason to take his account as factual. The most likely explanation is that it is the product of cryptomnesia—that he had in early years read or heard accounts of the Monmouth rebellion and life in Somerset during that period. Subsequently, having forgotten the specific sources of his information, he may have accepted the information as memory and elaborated it with personal detail (which would explain the apparent increase of memories with age).

CHILDHOOD MEMORIES

Quite different in kind and quality are the spontaneous memories of young children. A typical example is a·child who, upon learning to talk, begins speaking about persons, places, and events that have nothing to do with the present but seem to relate instead to another lifetime. As the child grows older, memories of that other life begin to fade, so that by the time the child reaches puberty, they are quite gone. Thereafter, anything the child knows about the former life comes from the tales of relatives about the "funny things" the child used to say.

Cases of this type, although certainly not the norm, are more frequent than one might suppose. Parents, upon hearing their child talk about the details of another life, tell the young person not to make up such stories. And thus corrected, the child becomes reluctant to share the memories with others and so ceases to speak of them.

In nonreincarnational cultures, talk about another lifetime is likely to be taken as fantastic lying or as incipient mental illness, and in either case is strongly discouraged. In reincarnational cultures, youthful memories of a past life are often considered to be unlucky, to portend an early death, or at the very least to be a source of difficulty in the family. Consequently, such memories tend to be suppressed wherever they occur.

One scholar, Ian Stevenson, Professor of Psychiatry at the University of Virginia, has devoted much of his professional career to studying cases of spontaneous memory that seem to indicate reincarnation. He has published the results of his work in a series of books, recounting the case histories and his efforts to check the facts behind them: *Twenty Cases Suggestive of Reincarnation, Cases of the Reincarnation Type* in three volumes, and a number of related works. Anyone who reads these case histories and the extraordinary facts that Stevenson has been able to verify must be impressed by his careful research methods and the accumulated evidence.

Stevenson's procedure is to get down the facts of the child's (or sometimes adult's) memory as soon as possible, to interview members of the family and neighbors to find out what they know about the events of the memory, to investigate whenever possible the scene of the remembered lifetime including persons from it who are still living, and to verify as many specific memories as possible. Stevenson has investigated thousands of cases of presumed memory. Many of these cases are insufficiently detailed to be convincing, but some are remarkably specific.

THE CASE OF IMAD

A typical but complex example is that of a young Lebanese boy named Imad, who when less than two years old began to talk about a previous life. He mentioned names of people he had known, described property he had owned, told of events which had happened. He sometimes spoke of these matters in his sleep, and sometimes in talking to himself he would wonder how those people he used to know were getting along now. He claimed to have been a member of the Bouhamzy family in the village of Khriby and begged to be taken there.

Imad's father scolded him for telling lies about a

former life. But one day a visitor from the village of Khriby came to Imad's town, and the young boy was able to identify him on the street. This event caused Imad's family to take his tales seriously. When Stevenson investigated the case, no contact had yet been made between Imad's present and former families. Although the two villages were only about fifteen miles apart, there was little social or commercial interchange between them.

The life that Imad seems to have remembered was that of Ibrahim Bouhamzy. Imad described Ibrahim's mistress, Jamileh, and was able to name and identify many of Ibrahim's relatives and friends. He described in detail a truck accident that killed one of Ibrahim's cousins. Imad described guns that had belonged to Ibrahim, who was fond of hunting. He described the location of Ibrahim's house, two adjacent wells, the garden under construction at the time of Ibrahim's death, three vehicles Ibrahim owned (a small yellow automobile, a bus, and a truck), and a variety of other details. He was able to repeat Ibrahim's dying words. Also significant is the fact that the child Imad often expressed great joy at being able to walk. Ibrahim died at about the age of twenty five after spending a year in a sanatorium; he suffered from tuberculosis and was bedridden for the last part of his life.

In trying to piece all of the information together into a coherent whole, Imad's family drew a number of wrong conclusions, which they attributed to young Imad. Because some of his earliest stories were about a man named Mahmoud, a truck accident in which the victim had both legs broken, and the beautiful woman Jamileh (her name being the first word Imad spoke), Imad's family mistakenly thought he was claiming to be Mahmoud and to have died in the truck accident, as well as to have had Jamileh as his wife. They made other wrong inferences about family relationships among the Bouhamzys and about the events Imad mentioned. Paradoxically, those errors are positive evidence in the case, for they show that Imad's family could not have been the source of the information behind his memories. Despite reservations sometimes expressed because of the confusion resulting from the misunderstandings by Imad's family, this case is a good one. Stevenson was able to investigate it and verify details relatively early, before Imad's family had made any contact with the Bouhamzys. Indeed, allowing for the difficulties inherent in investigating all cases of childhood memories, that of Imad seems to offer relatively strong evidence for reincarnation.

THE CASE OF JAGDISH CHANDRA

Another noteworthy case is that of Jagdish Chandra, who was born in 1923 in northern India. Shortly after his third birthday Jagdish began demanding that his father get his car for him. The family had no car, cars being uncommon among private persons at the time. When the father realized from other such remarks that his son was referring to things from a past life, he began to keep a diary of the boy's statements. Because of that record, this is one of the best documented cases of its kind.

Jagdish identified his former home as in Benares. He described the house in which he had lived in some detail, and specified that it was located near a ghat called Dash Ashwamadh, a broad flight of stairs leading down to the Ganges River. He reported his family name as Pandey. With such specific bits of information, Jagdish's father made efforts to confirm the facts, and discovered the family of the Pandeys in Benares, whose young son, Jai Gopal, had died a few years earlier.

Eventually his father took Jagdish to Benares, where the boy was able to lead his father to the Pandey house through the confusion of Benares streets and to identify various of Jai Gopal's relatives when he met them. When he was taken to the bathing ghat, Jagdish knew the procedures to be followed, even though his home was not near a river and he had no experience with the customs involved in bathing in the Ganges. Many other facts and behavior patterns seemed to identify Jadgish Chandra with Jai Gopal.

The refusal of the Pandey father to cooperate in the investigation was an impediment to its successful completion. But even that refusal turned out to be evidential. Jadgish remembered that his former father had once murdered a man and hidden his body in a well. If the memory was accurate, father Pandey could hardly be expected to assist in a line of inquiry that might be dangerous for him.

Stevenson investigated this case forty years after it happened, when Jagdish was an adult. Only the records kept and published by Jagdish's father make this a convincing case, but on their basis, it too is strong evidence for reincarnation.

NORMAL AND ABNORMAL REINCARNATION

Many of the cases that Stevenson investigated share some distinctive features. Typically the preceding life ended prematurely, by accident, violence, or illness. The time between lives was relatively brief. (In the case of Ibrahim-Imad, only nine years elapsed between the death of the former and the birth of the latter; and the interval is often less than that.) The two lives were in the same culture, often in the same general geographical area. And, of course, the child remembered the former life. These features reinforce one another.

According to many theosophical writers, when a life is completed normally, the experiences the lifetime was intended to hold for the incarnating individual have been fully realized. Then the individual needs a long period between lives to absorb and internalize the results of those experiences. When the individual returns to birth, it is to gain new experiences, and that return occurs after all the specific memories of the old personality have been discarded. There is thus no conscious link between the old and new personalities.

However, if a life is cut short before the individual has gained from it everything that was to have been experienced, the customary long period for digesting the past life is not needed. Also the hunger for life which drew the individual into incarnation has not been exhausted, as it would normally be during the course of a completed lifetime. Those two factors may lead to a quick reincarnation because there is nothing to keep the individual in the interim state, and the itch for life demands scratching. The individual is likely to be drawn back to the same neighborhood—to the same area and culture—with the aim of trying to complete the interrupted experience.

Normally during the long periods between lives, the old emotions, mind set, and memories are exhausted and discarded, so that when reincarnation eventually occurs, the former personality has been dispersed, and a new personality begins to develop afresh with the new body. In the case of a quick reincarnation, however, there has not been time for that process of wearing out and dispersing of the old to be completed. And so the individual comes back into birth bringing along some fragments of memory, and of desires and fears, from the former life.

Stevenson's cases, then, would be abnormal ones from the standpoint of the customary pattern of reincarnation. But it is their very abnormality that makes it possible to identify and study them. The normal pattern of reincarnation leaves no easily identifiable traces of a preceding life; the abnormal pattern does.

POSSIBLE EXPLANATIONS FOR "MEMORIES"

In investigating his cases, Stevenson considered a variety of possible explanations for the accuracy of the memories reported:

1. *Fraud.* Deliberate deceit is the least likely explanation in most cases. It would require an elaborate conspiracy between the children, their relatives, neighbors, strangers in other cities, and so on. Furthermore, the presumed conspirators normally had nothing to gain—they had no motive. Parents were often extremely reluctant to accept such memories.

2. *Cryptomnesia.* It is possible to believe quite firmly that we have experienced something we have actually read or been told about, but which our mind has converted into a memory. Such hidden (Greek *crypto-*) memory *(mnesia)* is also responsible for the phenomenon of unconscious plagiarism—a writer may store away a particularly appealing phrase or sentence read some where, and then come to think of it as one he or she has composed. Part of what Stevenson investigated was whether anyone in contact with the child knew about the matters the child reported as memory.

3. *Telepathy with the living.* Possibly the children were reading the minds of living persons who had knowledge of the events and then converting that information into pseudo memories.

4. *Retrocognition or precognition.* Another possibility is that the child, by some extraordinary faculty, was directly aware of events in the past, before its birth (retrocognition). Or perhaps the child, by an even more

extraordinary faculty, was somehow aware of the facts that the investigator would uncover in the future and was predicting them (precognition).

5. *Telepathy with the dead.* Perhaps the child had entered into telepathic contact with the consciousness of a deceased person and was misperceiving the information thus gained as its own memories.

6. *Possession.* Perhaps the child was in fact possessed by the spirit of the dead person and the memories reported were the actual memories of that other consciousness who was co-dwelling in the body or who had replaced the original personality.

Possibilities 3 through 6 are increasingly improbable from the standpoint of ordinary science and, while not impossible, would require a revolution in scientific thinking just as great as the acceptance of reincarnation as an explanation. Finally, then, Stevenson concluded that the seventh possibility was sometimes the most likely one:

7. *Reincarnation.* The memories are what they seem to be—recollections of events from a past life of the child.

Stevenson never claims that his cases "prove" reincarnation, certainly not in the popular sense of that term. The evidence is hard to come by and hard to evaluate. All Stevenson claims is that these cases suggest reincarnation as an explanation and that there is no more probable explanation available for them. That is a modest claim, but still a remarkable one for an academic scientist to make. Since Stevenson's work, it is no longer correct to say that there is no real, solid evidence for reincarnation. That is exactly what he has supplied.

9

What Reincarnates?

*I*f reincarnation seems likely because of its explanatory value and the evidence of memories about past lives, the question of how it works naturally arises. That question is examined in this and the following two chapters, beginning here with the question of what exactly it is that reincarnates.

One possible answer to the question of what reincarnates is that nothing does. That is, there is no permanent self that carries over from one lifetime to the next. Rather, each lifetime creates causes that cannot be fully worked out during that lifetime, so those causes generate another life-form, which inherits them. Only the causes can be said to reincarnate, not any entity behind them. That is the answer given by Buddhism, in accordance with the Buddha's teaching that there is no abiding self in anything in the universe *(anatta)*.

However, other varieties of reincarnationism do suppose that there is an underlying entity, an essential self, that expresses itself from time to time through a physical form. The answer given here to the question of what reincarnates is of the latter type. It is based on teachings in the theosophical tradition, which dates in modern times from the foundation of the Theosophical Society in 1875 by a Russian noblewoman, Helena Petrovna

Blavatsky; an American lawyer and military man, Colonel Henry Steel Olcott; an Irish-American lawyer, William Quan Judge; and a few others.

The modern theosophical tradition is derived partly from the Wisdom literature of the East and the West—the Upanishads and other sacred scriptures of India, the Neoplatonic teachings of the Classical world, some Gnostic treatises of early Christianity. It is also derived partly from the teachings given by several Eastern sages to the founders of the Society. In addition, it has been influenced by the personal research of several generations of theosophists, who have attempted to investigate theosophical teachings by such means as were available to them—normal and paranormal.

Because of its mixed origins, what is described here is presented neither as dogma to be accepted on faith nor as scientifically demonstrable conclusions. Rather, these explanations are offered as part of a unified view of life—the theosophical worldview—which forms a coherent whole and gives an account of life that many have found reasonable and sustaining. Individual teachings that cannot be verified independently need to be judged as part of such a total view.

BODY AND SOUL, PERSONALITY AND INDIVIDUALITY

In speaking about reincarnation, we often talk about the reincarnating entity (the "soul") and its body as though the former "put on" the latter, like a person getting dressed in a suit or coat. Indeed that very analogy has often been used to describe the relationship of "soul" and body. It is useful for some purposes, but it may also mislead. It is an analogy that reflects the dominant Western religious view of the human constitution as having two components—a body and a soul.

In early Christianity, Saint Paul talked about three

components—body, soul, and spirit. This Pauline analysis can be interpreted in various ways; one is to regard spirit as the deepest awareness within us and soul as the emotional-mental complex of faculties that spirit uses to express itself through the body. Paul also recognized that there could be more than one sort of body—the ordinary fleshly body (of the Old Adam) and a spiritualized, glorified body that was not subject to the limitations of the physical matter we know. However, this more sophisticated anatomy of our constitution was abandoned by the later Church for the simpler, dualistic one. Although serviceable for some purposes, the dualistic view is woefully inadequate for any use that requires a complex view of human nature.

Clearly it is not adequate to say that the soul reincarnates in new bodies. For in this dualistic view, the soul is usually taken to include mind, consciousness, memory, self-identity, and indeed most of the components of our personality. But it is obviously not the personality that reincarnates. The personality is intimately connected with the body, and is therefore developed anew in each incarnation along with the new body.

When Theosophy makes a twofold division of the human constitution, it is not into body and soul, but rather into personality and individuality, which are our two "selves." The personality is what we think of as "us" in any given lifetime. It is a product of the impulses we have received from our own past lives, the genetic inheritance from our parents, and the environmental influences exerted on us during this lifetime. It is the aggregate of our body, vital energy, sensations, perceptions, emotions, reasoning, subconscious mind, memories, anticipations, imaginations, and fantasies. It is what we symbolize by our name. In a word, it is "us," as we usually think of ourselves.

The individuality is more difficult to describe. It is

the ability to think that underlies any particular thoughts the personality has. It is the structure of the mind, as distinct from the way the personality uses that structure to interact with the world. It is an ability, only latent in most of us, to know directly how others think and feel. It is a spark from the flame of the one Life of the universe. To our personality, the individuality seems like another and higher being. Indeed, one of the poetic terms used for it is the "Holy Guardian Angel."

In the theosophical view, the individuality is what incarnates—the personality is what is incarnated. They are both us, but the personality is our temporary self for one lifetime, whereas the individuality is the impersonal, essential self that links all our lifetimes, like beads on a string.

SEVEN PRINCIPLES

Instead of any twofold or threefold division, Theosophy often uses a sevenfold analysis of the human constitution. The seven components are called *principles* and consist of the following (a Sanskrit term often used in theosophical writings is given in parentheses):

1. The ultimate Self *(atma)*. This principle is a spark of the one Life of the universe. In its essence it is identical with the ultimate reality of the cosmos and thus does not "belong" to any individual separately. It is the divine core of our being and of all beings. Because it is common to all of us, we are all united at the deepest level of our being.

2. Intuition, wisdom, compassion *(buddhi)*. This is a faculty latent in most human beings and fully active only in a few of the most advanced of our kind, the great spiritual leaders of humanity. When active, it is the means of making direct contact with other beings, not

by words or sight, but spirit to spirit. That direct contact brings with it complete understanding, full knowledge, perfect wisdom. And since to know all is to forgive all, it also brings perfect empathy and compassion.

Even when not active, the buddhi has a function: to "support" or "contain" the atma. Taken together these two principles are called the *monad* (Greek for 'unity'), the basis of consciousness in us. The monad does not, in itself, belong to any individual. It is rather in all beings as a kind of collective oversoul, the common ground of our existence. That one existence in all beings is, however, individualized by the next principle, which by "containing" or "reflecting" the monad creates the continuing individuality which reincarnates.

3. Mind *(manas).* The mind has two aspects because it participates in both the individuality and the personality:

a. Pure or "higher" mind. This aspect of the mind is our ability to think and is the pattern by which the mind is structured. It includes what we term the "laws of logic." It is referred to here as "pure mind" because it is unmixed with personal concerns or experiences. It is also what makes us individuals, like a cup holding some portion of the universal monad in it. It preserves the essence of what we learn from each incarnation and is thus the link between all our lives. It is particularly what incarnates.

The mind is like the Roman god Janus, the god of doors and of the new year, to whom the month January was sacred. Janus was depicted as having two faces on opposite sides of his head because he could see both forwards and backwards. The mind similarly has two faces, one looking toward the monad, the universal one Life in us, and the other looking toward the personality, the particular manifestation of our life in the world. It has

also been called the bridge between the individuality
and the personality. According to Theosophy, when we
incarnate, the pure mind sends a ray of itself into the
brain of the developing new body, and thus forms the
personal mind of that life, the other aspect of mind.

b. Brain or "lower" mind. This second aspect of the
mind is what we usually mean when we talk about our
mind. It is built up gradually during our lifetime, based
on the physical characteristics of the brain, the environmental influences that come to bear on us, and the
impulse given to it by the pure mind. It is the means
for processing and recalling our thoughts. It is where
we have our sense of I-ness. It, more than any other principle, is what we identify as "us." It is also closely linked
with the next principle.

4. Desire, passion, emotional feeling *(kama)*. This
principle is that in us which likes and dislikes things.
It has attractions and repulsions. It forms attachments.
It loves and hates. It is the basis of all emotions and the
motive power behind all actions. Because this principle is sometimes rather violent in its expression and is
always irrational, it has a bad reputation. But it is essential to life.

As the source of our motivation, desire is an important and positive aspect of our being. When it is well
attuned, it not only responds to the world of sensations,
but also resonates with the deepest intuitions within us.
Thus like the mind, with which it forms an interrelated
whole during incarnation, it has two aspects.

The equivalent among the ancient Greeks for kama
was the god Eros, desire. They said that there are really two such deities—a heavenly and an earthy one. The
heavenly Eros was responsible for the world's coming
into existence, and he was the source of all order and
relationship in the world. The earthy Eros was respon-

sible for physical attraction and sexual love among creatures. But the two gods Eros, like the two aspects of kama, are just two different functions of the same force—one acting on the cosmic stage and the other on a personal one. So there is nothing inherently bad about desire. We couldn't have a world without it.

5. Life energy, vital force, libido (*prana*, literally 'breath'). This principle is sometimes called *jiva*, which means 'life.' It is the subtle "juices" in us, the vital electricity that powers our psychic engine. Its proper flow is essential to sound health of body and mind. When the supply of energy is low or its current is sluggish, we feel "down." When it is abundant and vigorous, we are "up." The flow of energy is partly automatic, responding to conditions in the world around us, and is partly influenced by our likes and dislikes (kama). When it is absent, a body is dead.

6. Subtle body, called "astral" in early theosophical literature and "etheric" later (*linga sharira*, of which "characteristic or distinctive form" is a literal translation). In addition to the physical body that we can perceive with our ordinary senses, there is another aspect of the body, made also of matter, but of a more rarefied kind. The life energy flows through it, and it provides the model, or template, according to which the physical body develops. It is sometimes called the "double," but it would be more accurate to say that the next principle, the physical body, is the double of this characteristic form.

7. Dense form, physical body (*sthula sharira*). This is our ordinary physical body. It is Hamlet's "too, too solid flesh," but it is also the basis of our personality, the foundation of our life in the physical world, the expression of all our other principles, and therefore of no little importance.

The first three of these seven principles are a triad corresponding to the individuality: ultimate self, intuition, and pure mind. The other four are a quaternary corresponding to the personality: the linked brain-mind and desire, life energy, subtle body, and physical body. The significant thing about this sevenfold analysis, however, is that according to it we are composite beings. There is no single, separate, abiding core that is really "us."

The theosophical view accords with the Buddhist teaching of *anatta*, when the latter is understood as saying that we are not eternally distinct entities, but rather manifestations in time and space of the one "Be-ness" or absolute reality. That is, there is no "little person" inside us that is our real identity—our separate, eternal "soul" in the usual sense of that term. Rather we are a complex of faculties or principles, comparable to the Buddhist skandhas. Those that constitute the personality are fashioned anew each lifetime and are thus temporary. The monad, consisting of the ultimate Self and the intuition, is the basis of our existence, but in itself is impersonal and unindividualized.

The closest thing in us to an abiding core-self is the pure mind. It individualizes the monad in each of us and is the unit of reincarnation. That combination of pure mind and monad is referred to in theosophical literature as the Ego (Latin for 'I'). This theosophical use of *Ego* is related to, but distinct from, the general psychological use of the term with an initial small letter, *ego*.

All of us identify something within ourselves that is "us"—which we think of as the real us, the center of our being. We may locate that feeling of me-ness or ego in our physical body, vital functions, emotions, or brain-minds. The reincarnating self, of course, is not any of those. So the theosophical use of Ego is intended to remind us that it is best to identify the center of our being not with any of the more transitory parts of our nature, but with that which endures across lives. The importance of making the right identification will appear in the next chapter, in which we consider our experiences after death.

Although the pure mind is the basis of our sense of separate identity, it is not an independent consciousness; it is rather a vehicle for the one consciousness in all life. It is long-lasting, continuing over many lifetimes, linking a series of historical personalities together as "me." During our series of personal lives, it is the basis of our "higher," "core," or "essential" self, our individuality, which is a Presence the mystic knows, the Overself. But finally it too is temporary—merely a complex that allows the one Self, the ultimate Self of us all, to play the game of life. We are complex beings, not simple souls.

FIVE VEHICLES

Speaking of the mind, not as consciousness itself, but as a vehicle through which consciousness functions suggests yet another and complementary way of looking at the human constitution and thus at what reincarnates. The principles just described are a mixed lot. They are bodies of denser and subtler grades of matter, energy, passions, a mind, and some spiritual elements that are rather hard to talk about. They do not seem to be all the same sort of thing. The complementary way of looking at our make-up offers more consistency.

In this last way, there is a basic unit of consciousness in us, the monad. That unit of consciousness expresses itself simultaneously through a number of vehicles composed of different grades of matter. The world does not consist only of the kind of matter of which we are normally aware. In addition to dense physical matter, there are said to be progressively finer grades of stuff, of which five are important to the present discussion.

Many things which we usually think of as immaterial—energies, emotions, thoughts, aspirations—can also be thought of as forms or vibrations in various of the subtler grades of matter. That concept, although very strange when Theosophy first began to teach it, should not seem so odd today, for now it is a commonplace of physics that energy and mass (or matter, loosely speaking) are equivalent. The barriers between the material and the nonmaterial have broken down.

So one of the early Eastern teachers put a rhetorical question to a student: "But is there, I ask, either a sensation, an abstract idea, a tendency of mind, or a mental power, that one could call an absolutely non-molecular phenomenon?" (*Mahatma Letters* 109). And on other occasions he wrote, "We believe in MATTER alone, in matter as visible nature and matter in its invisibility" (56), and "Thoughts are things—have tenacity, coherence, and life. . . they are real entities" (49). Theosophy holds that there are kinds of matter other than physical and that what we usually think of as immaterial thoughts and emotions are actually phenomena in such subtle matter.

We can think of subtle grades of matter in a variety of ways. For example, we might think of them as being essentially like the matter we know, but so much rarer in structure that our physical senses do not perceive them. Modern physics has taught us that even physical stuff is at bottom something quite different from what our senses lead us to believe. Viewed on the atomic and subatomic levels, the densest and most inert physical matter is mostly empty space with quanta of energy blinking on and off in disconcertingly unpredictable ways. It does not take much imagination to conceive of other manifestations of that same energy as other forms of matter with properties different from those of ordinary physical stuff.

We can also think of those kinds of matter as "fields," that is, regions of the multidimensional space of the cosmos in which some characteristic forces or properties operate. Such fields are not separate from each other; they can and do interpenetrate. Within the same area of three-dimensional space, many different fields can coexist. Gravitation is one such field and is, indeed, perhaps the key field for defining what we mean by the physical world and matter. Other fields may define other kinds of worlds and other sorts of matter, all interpenetrating and affecting us, each in its own way.

However we conceive of such alternative realities, we are using metaphors to help us realize something that is out of our normal experience. There is nothing wrong with using metaphor; human beings have always done so, and modern science still does it. We must be careful, however, not to mistake a metaphor for the fact behind it.

Of various kinds of matter or fields, five are relevant to reincarnation. They are often called "planes," and that metaphorical term will be used here, with the caution that we must not be misled by it into thinking of the realities it represents as being tiers like the layers of a cake or the strata of a geological deposit. We have a vehicle or body composed of the matter of each plane, through which we make contact with that plane. These vehicles are also called the "aura" because clairvoyants have described them as radiant nimbuses surrounding the physical body. The unit consciousness of the monad functions on the following planes through the corresponding vehicles:

1. "Higher" mental plane and causal body. These cor-

respond to the principle of pure mind. The vehicle is referred to as a *causal* body because, as the center of our individuality, it is the cause of all our personalities.

2. "Lower" mental plane and mental body. These correspond to the principle of brain-mind.

3. Emotional (sometimes called "astral") plane and body. These correspond to the principle of desire.

4. Vital (sometimes called "etheric" or also "astral") plane and body. These correspond to the two principles of the subtle body and the life energy.

5. Dense physical plane and body. These are the world we ordinarily perceive and the physical body through which we perceive it.

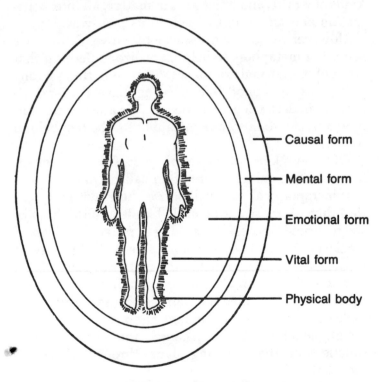

Causal form

Mental form

Emotional form

Vital form

Physical body

THE HUMAN CONSTITUTION

Common	Pauline	Selves	Principles	Consciousness and Vehicles
soul	spirit	individuality Ego higher Self	ultimate self (atma)	unit consciousness (monad)
			intuition (buddhi)	
			pure mind (manas)	higher mental (causal) body
	soul		brain-mind (manas)	lower mental body
			desires (kama)	emotional body
	body	personality ego lower self	life energy (prana)	vital body
			characteristic form (linga sharira)	
body			dense form (sthula sharira)	physical body

CONSTITUENTS OF THE HUMAN CONSTITUTION

According to the theosophical explanation, the unitary consciousness, dwelling in the causal body as our individuality, incarnates by gathering to itself matter on the other planes and forming new bodies out of them— mental, emotional, vital, and dense physical bodies. Those bodies collectively constitute the personality of a new lifetime. At the end of life, after the death of the physical body, the other bodies are gradually discarded and disintegrate; the personality disappears, and the individuality is left to begin again the process of incarnation.

CONCLUSION

This chapter has sketched several ways of looking at the human constitution, including three approaches found in the Wisdom Tradition and modern theosophical writings: (1) a duality of temporary personality and longer abiding individuality, (2) a septenary of principles, (3) a unit of consciousness expressing itself through five vehicles. These various ways of looking at ourselves are just alternative views of the same reality. Which of them we adopt is a question of usefulness—whether we think of ourselves as twofold (an individual and a personal self), as a complex of seven principles, or as consciousness functioning through five vehicles.

In general, what things are depends on how it is useful to think of them. Physicists talk about light sometimes as though it consisted of very small particles, at other times as though it were waves in some substance. It is no good asking physicists, "Which is light *really*—a particle or a wave?" They can't tell us. They can only say that light behaves in some ways as though it were particles and in others as though it were waves. How we think of it will depend on what is most useful at any given time.

So we can also think of the human constitution variously, as a duality of two selves, as seven principles, or as consciousness and five vehicles, depending on which is most useful at a given time. However, in respect to the question of what reincarnates, with which this chapter has been primarily concerned, the three models of our constitution say much the same thing:

1. The individual self, which is an expression of the one Life of the universe and lasts through all our successive lifetimes, manifests by incarnating as a personality, which endures for only one lifetime.

2. The triad of ultimate self, intuition, and pure mind manifests by incarnating as the quaternary of brain-mind and desire, life energy, subtle body, and dense body.

3. The unitary consciousness of the monad individualized by the causal body expresses itself in the mental, emotional, vital, and physical worlds by incarnating in vehicles appropriate to those worlds.

The terms and classifications differ, but the reality behind them is the same. Whether light is a particle or a wave, it shines.

The next two chapters deal with the process by which these selves, principles, or bodies take part in the cycle of life and death, beginning with the event of death.

10

What Happens When We Die?

Although the human being is complex and composite, made up of various principles, we normally perceive ourselves as a single whole. Indeed, mental health requires the identification of a single center, the ego or personal self, within the complex of our psyche. The need for a sense of wholeness applies to both life and death, although after death we may be forced into a reassessment of who or what we are.

The theosophical tradition has a good deal to say about the state of the after-life and the conditions between incarnations. Moreover, what it says has recently been confirmed in two ways. First, studies have been done of the experiences of persons who have nearly died but survived and retained a recollection of what it was like to be on the verge of death. Second, hypnotically induced regressions to the state between lives have been conducted.

NEAR-DEATH EXPERIENCES

Recent investigations into near-death experiences suggest that Shakespeare was wrong when he spoke of "that undiscovered country from whose bourne no traveler returns." A fair number of persons have traveled to the boundary of the Land of Death and have returned to tell quite a lot about it. In these cases a person has come close to dying, sometimes actually being pronounced dead, and then has been revived. Upon regaining physical consciousness, he or she may remember experiences from the near-death event.

Such near-death experiences have become the subject of intensive study by several investigators, notably Elisabeth Kübler-Ross, Raymond A. Moody, Kenneth Ring, and Michael B. Sabom. These researchers have interviewed persons who came back from apparent death with memories of that state. Out of the many cases they have studied, a common core of memories emerges, which has been called the "near-death experience."

Those memories often have a profound effect on the person, making a radical alteration in attitude toward life and death and one's fellow human beings. The experience itself is by no means a frightening one. Those who have undergone it regard the prospect of their eventual death with calmness and a complete lack of fear.

Those who have lived through the experience also find they cannot adequately put it into words. It involves a sense of timelessness but also of increased reality. It is not like a dream or hallucination, but rather is described as being realer than real. The subjects know they are dying, but lose all sense of pain and distress. They feel happiness and even elation. If such near-death experiences are typical of what all of us will go through when we finally die, they are of considerable interest.

Hundreds of cases have now been examined, among which a remarkable consistency has been noted. The experiences are by no means identical; they differ in detail, in the events they include, and often in the order of those events. The accompanying sense of timelessness means that the order perceived is thematic rather than chronological.

The experience has two main aspects. One is located in the vicinity of the dying body, as the experiencer looks down on that body and is aware of events going on around it. The other is transcendental and located in a symbolic setting. The elements of the two aspects, which may be intermixed, are as follows.

1. The experience may be introduced by a noise—a whistling wind or a rushing, ringing sound.

2. There is a sense of profound peace and well-being, an absence of all pain and anxiety.

3. The dying person becomes aware of separation from the body and sees the room, including his or her own body, as if looking down from above, as though from the ceiling.

4. The dying person looks on at events going on near the body and hears discussions by doctors and nurses or those around the deathbed. The accuracy of such reports has been confirmed in a number of cases. The dying are aware of their surroundings, but they are no longer in the body, which is unconscious.

5. The consciousness, freed from the physical body, seems to have some other sort of body and finds that it can travel to other places simply by thinking of them.

6. The dying person undergoes a life review, like a rapid motion picture played either forward or in reverse or sometimes not chronologically but according to a thematic order.

7. The dying person enters a great darkness—a tunnel or a void.

8. At the end of the tunnel or somewhere in the void, a light appears and grows. The light becomes intensely brilliant but not distressing—quite the contrary, it is a light of revelation.

9. The dying person enters the world of the light—a realm of surpassing brightness and beauty. This world may be a meadow with flowers or some other realistic

place but is always appealingly beautiful. There is an ancient tradition of the paradise from which we come and to which we return as a *locus amoenus*, or 'pleasant place.' That tradition coincides perfectly with this aspect of the near-death experience.

10. There is an encounter with someone. The dying person may feel a presence or hear a voice or see a figure. Sometimes the encounter is with a long-dead relative or friend. Sometimes the presence is a godlike figure—the expectations of the dying person seem to form the specific shape of the presence. Those who anticipate going to the arms of Jesus may find him waiting.

11. The dying person is told that a decision has to be made whether to return to life or to continue into the state of death. Often the presence urges a return. There may be a barrier or limit which the dying person must either cross over or turn back from.

12. The decision to return is made, often reluctantly. Sometimes the return happens involuntarily, with a sense of being pushed.

Not all of those interviewed about near-death experiences have gone through all twelve stages, but everything they reported fits into the scheme. These near-death experiences are, of course, not death. The person who has them always survives. But these accounts suggest what the beginning of death may be like—what the first few steps on the other side will be. For a continuation of the story, we must turn to other sources.

THE BARDO REMEMBERED UNDER HYPNOSIS

In the Tibetan tradition, the state between lives is called the *bardo*, and that term has therefore been used by a Toronto psychiatrist, Joel L. Whitton, in his book *Life between Life*, coauthored with Joe Fisher. While using past-life regression in his psychiatric practice,

Whitton discovered that some patients appeared also to remember details of their existence between earthly lives. To a considerable extent, the between-life state reported by Whitton's patients and other hypnotic subjects resembles that of the near-death experience. But there are some significant additional details.

Whitton's patients comment on a sense of impersonality in the bardo state, in contrast to both the near-death experience and past-life regression. One reported, "In experiencing a past life one sees oneself as a distinct personality which engenders an emotional reaction. In the interlife there's no part of me I can see. I'm an observer surrounded by images" (53).

The extent of self-consciousness in the bardo seems to vary with the person. Those who have been concerned with their spiritual development during life are conscious during the between-life state; those who have focused their attention on earthly concerns exclusively are inclined to sleep through the bardo.

Others confirm a sense of timelessness in the afterlife, in which there is no succession but rather a "collage of simultaneity." The dead seem to be aware of sequence only just upon leaving earthly life or just upon reentering it. Time as we know it is not a characteristic of the afterlife.

The tunnel, the light, and the beautiful place are all reported from the bardo. Also one's thoughts and expectations seem to shape the environment of the bardo, as they do the world of the near-death experience.

Whitton's subjects reported encounters with what he calls a "Board of Judgment," typically consisting of three figures who help the deceased to make an impartial, but benevolent and encouraging judgment of the past life. The process of judgment is accompanied by a review of the past life, and there is also a planning session during which the individual lays out the course of the coming life and makes choices about it.

The theme of judgment appears in most of the world's traditions about the afterlife. In ancient Egypt, the dead soul was weighed against the feather of truth, and in Zoroastrianism the soul is judged while balanced upon a bridge spanning the gap between earth and heaven. The trinity of figures governing destiny is familiar also from the three Fates of Greek mythology and the Germanic Norns (reflected in Macbeth's three weird sisters—*weird* originally meaning 'fate').

The experiences of Whitton's patients match very well those reported by persons who have undergone the near-death experience and also theosophical traditions about the afterlife, which are described below. The similarities can hardly be accidental. Some of his patients were doubtless familiar with such other descriptions and so may have been influenced by them or by Whitton's own ideas on the subject. It is also possible, however, that all these descriptions are of the same reality and therefore are similar.

TEACHINGS OF THE WISDOM TRADITION

Within the theosophical tradition there are several accounts of the after-death state, which reflect various possible experiences as well as the interests and mindsets of those who have given the accounts. The following description is a blending of several versions. Because the expectations of a dying person strongly influence the after-death experience, there may be still other possibilities than that sketched here.

As our physical body dies and just before our brain fails, our memory becomes acute and thorough, and we make a rapid review of the events of our past life. As some who have been through it but survived have said, "My whole life flashed before my eyes." This is the life review of the near-death experience. It allows us to see our life as a whole and to put its various events into perspective. It is an opportunity to decide how well we have fulfilled the intentions we had before we took birth. During the review we assess the accomplishments of our past life—not as a matter of either blame or self-congratulation, but as a personal observation of what we have done.

At the moment the physical body dies, the vital (or subtle) body separates permanently from it. The two are connected by a strand of rarefied matter like a cord or thread. During life, in various states of unconsciousness such as sleep or under anesthesia, the vital body may separate from the dense physical body, but is always connected by the cord. At death the cord breaks. Then the vital life energy is dissipated, and the consciousness passes into another dimension of being. The barrier of the near-death experience has been passed.

If the newly dead retain an awareness of their surroundings, they may be disoriented, dazed by the experience. They may not realize that a barrier has been crossed because the world in which they find themselves looks much like the physical plane they have just left. But gradually they recognize that they are in a new state, a different dimension of reality. In gaining that recognition, the newly dead person may be aided by "helpers," other dead persons or living persons who can function in that other dimension during sleep. These helpers are like the friends or relatives encountered in the near-death experience. Their function is to assist the newly dead in making the transition.

As part of that transition, the emotional and mental principles disengage themselves from the vital body, which is left to hover in the vicinity of the physical corpse—both of the latter now being cast-off vehicles of consciousness. Those bodies gradually disintegrate, although cremation hastens the process and hygienically destroys the remains, both physical and psychic.

During this stage of the afterlife, the elements that make up what is left of our personality are gradually dissociated from the essential self, whose expression they were, and are reorganized. It is as though various substances had been dissolved in a liquid and now are being crystalized or precipitated out, each one gravitating to the level that is appropriate to it. Our psyche—which during life is a jumble of impulses, emotions, thoughts, sensations, and identities—now is divided into two major parts.

All our thoughts and emotions that are purely personal and identified solely with the past life clump together as a surrounding shell, like the husk of a fruit or the cocoon woven by a caterpillar. However, the other part of us—our unselfish impulses, all that is generous and noble in us, all that is altruistic and worthy—is being absorbed into the spiritual core of our being, the essential self within us (the pure mind connected to the monad).

That process of absorption has been called a "gestation" period. What is gestating is our real self, as the fruits of our past life are incorporated into the abiding core of our being (the individuality). It is the transformation of the caterpillar into a butterfly, waiting to come forth from its cocoon into the light of an idealized world.

The process of separating the more and less worthy elements within us is referred to as a "struggle." Just as the butterfly must struggle to free itself from its chrysalis before it can fly away, so the individuality must free itself from the limitations of its old personality, keeping only what it can transform and abandoning the rest. The chrysalis becomes an abandoned shell of our old personality, which we no longer need. The butterfly is our true individuality, which survives many deaths, always growing in wisdom and compassion.

The intensity of the struggle depends on what we have identified with during life. If we have thought of ourselves primarily as our body, vital functions, and personal emotions and thoughts, the struggle may be vigorous and prolonged, for we will be unwilling to leave what we have accepted for so long as ourselves—that would seem to be a second death. We will then grasp the shell of our personal self and resist separation from it. On the other hand, to the extent that we have identified ourselves with a larger sense of self, with impersonal and altruistic emotions and thoughts, the struggle will be easier and shorter, for we will already have made the identification that death demands.

It is for this reason that the theosophical term *Ego* is applied to the "higher self"—the pure mind, as it reflects the intuition and ultimate One Self. If we identify that as the "me" or ego in us, we greatly aid the postmortem process and speed up our evolution. The purpose of meditation is to identify our ego with the greater, less personal aspects of our being. Meditation is thus a kind of little death, in which our personal self is gradually accustomed to ceasing to be. Through such practice we gain the realization that we are not really that personal self, but something far greater—more splendid, more inclusive, and more abiding—something integrated with the whole cosmos and all other beings.

There is some difference of opinion about how long the process of the shell formation, gestation, and struggle lasts and about how conscious we are during it. H. P. Blavatsky, in speaking of this period, says, "After the dissolution of the body, there commences for it (Ego) a period of full awakened consciousness, or a state of chaotic dreams or an utterly dreamless sleep undistinguishable from annihilation" (*Key* 111). That would suggest that the degree of consciousness varies with different persons and the amount of preparation made during life.

It is said that after the individuality or Ego has sepa-
rated from its shell, it again reviews the events of the
past life, this time from a perspective unsullied by personal bias. It makes an impartial overview of the life
just past and thereby chooses which of the experiences
of that life are to be retained in its memory for the next
stage of the afterlife, dismissing the rest. Thus the individual self enters the next stage, known as *devachan*,
the heaven world.

Devachan is purely subjective, a vivid dream-like state
in which everything is exactly as the dreaming self would
want it to be. It is a world of perfect illusion, in which
there are no frustrations, no unhappiness, no bitter-
ness—only joy, and fulfillment, and satisfaction. It is
a reflection of the best and highest in us—selfless love,
pure abstract thought, heroism, our deepest insights—
played out on an inner screen. Experiencing our individuality in this way, purified of the pull of the personality, strengthens our finest qualities.

Devachan is the experience symbolized by the *locus
amoenus*, the pleasant place, of tradition, and fore-
shadowed in the near-death experience. If the gestation
period is a kind of purgatory, in which we are purged
of the dross of our personalities and cleansed from the
irrelevant aspects of our past life, devachan is our
reward. It is consolation and comfort. It is rest and relax-
ation from the problems of incarnate life. The exact nature of the devachanic experience varies with each
individual, for in it each of us has what we individual-
ly want.

The statement that devachan is a dream state or world
of illusion does not imply that it is therefore unreal. In
a sense all of existence is unreal and dream-like. The external world of everyday life is a great illusion, for
nothing is really what it seems to be here. The chief difference between the physical world of active life and
devachan is that in this world we do not control the il-

lusion directly. Objective reality is an enforced illusion that we share.

In devachan, all individuals build the illusions that they want, and there is no conflict between illusions, for all space in this dimension is subjective. The world of devachan is the world made perfect, modeled exactly as we would have it. According to H. P. Blavatsky, there is no punishment in the after-life, no hell, only recompense and recuperation. The rough place is earth, and after it we need a little respite. The purpose of devachan is to give that comfort and consolation—a breathing space between rounds of active life on earth, during which we can absorb the results of the past life and prepare for the next.

Nothing that is ignoble or discordant can enter devachan. The skandhas, those predispositions that influence what we are during an incarnation, cannot enter, but wait, as it were, on the threshold of devachan for the return of the individual. They have been called the "elements of limited existence" because without them the individual in devachan exercises a full, unlimited range of abilities. When we return to birth, however, we again come under the influence of the skandhas and the limitations of earthly life.

Eventually we do return. Having been fully comforted by the consolations of devachan, we begin to hunger again for life. For a cyclical pattern governs all life and death. We eat a meal to nourish our body and then spend a while digesting it. As the digestion ends, we feel hunger pangs telling us it is time to eat again. So too during life we gain experience which must be digested and absorbed during the devachan state. But after we have incorporated within our permanent selves (our "causal bodies") the nourishing experiences of our previous life, we feel the need to return to the world for more experience.

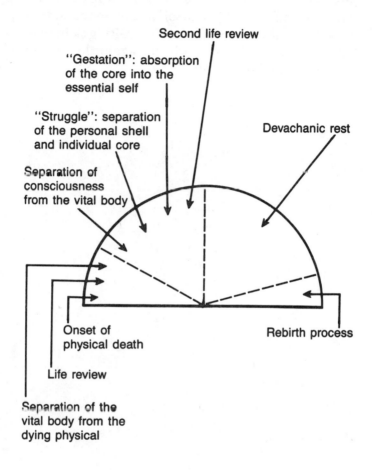

Second life review

"Gestation": absorption
of the core into the
essential self

"Struggle": separation
of the personal shell
and individual core

Devachanic rest

Separation of
consciousness
from the vital body

Onset of
physical death

Rebirth process

Life review

Separation of the
vital body from the
dying physical

STAGES OF THE AFTER-DEATH STATE

With the return of the hunger for existence in the physical world, the self slips out of its realistic dream into a dreamless sleep, a state of unconsciousness. It turns back to the physical world and its waiting skandhas, to enter into a new body and begin again the process of forming a new personality.

11

What Happens When We Are Reborn?

As our essential self absorbs the useful experiences of the past life—lives them over again in memory, sees their implications, realizes their benefits, builds them into the fabric of our being, having sloughed off whatever was ephemeral about them—we take the long devachanic rest from the activities of personal life. What the condition of the essential self may be in its own sphere, without personal limits, we cannot imagine, anymore than an infant can imagine the concerns and actions of a mature adult. It is a realm of being too different from that of our personal lives for us to conceive except by poetic descriptions.

How long the devachanic vacation from personhood lasts depends on many factors. Among them are the length and richness of experience of the past life and the availability of a suitable body and appropriate circumstances for the next life. It is said to be usual for the interval between lives to last for hundreds of years—sometimes less but sometimes considerably longer. Herodotus said the ancient Egyptians believed the period between births was thousands of years long. On the other hand, recent investigations report a much shorter time. It is likely, as suggested in chapter 4, that the average interval between lives may vary in different historical epochs, depending on the richness of experiences available in the world.

However long the interval, eventually a time comes when the essential self can no longer resist another period of personal expression and experience. We are overcome by a hunger for life, a thirst for experience. We itch to be born, and we must scratch.

The Process of Rebirth

When the essential self reaches a critical point in its impulse to be reborn, it sends forth a part of itself into the worlds of denser matter, around which regather the materials of its inner vehicles or subtle "bodies," conditioned by its past lives. Then it awaits an appropriate vehicle of birth.

We might compare it to a beam of light shot out into the night from a covered flame. It plays about in the darkness on this form and that, flickering over the shapes, until it falls upon a suitable one. The heredity must be right, the environmental conditions must be right, and the connections must be right—that is, the essential self needs to be born in the company of other selves whom it has known from the past to resume relationships and work out karma.

When the essential self is drawn to the right situation, it begins the process of entering into it. What goes on during that process has been described by the clairvoyant Geoffrey Hodson, and also discussed by H. P. Blavatsky and others such as James S. Perkins. Joel L. Whitton's accounts of existence between incarnations, based on the hypnotically induced memories of his patients and experimental subjects, also deal with the process. The following account is based on their descriptions, with some of the gaps filled in by inference.

Just before birth, the self has a vision of the life which is to come. This prospective vision, which is mentioned by H. P. Blavatsky, Plato, and *The Tibetan Book of the*

Dead, is the complement of the life review that follows death. During the preview, we have an overview of what is karmically arranged for the next life, of the conditions we will encounter, and of the responses that are appropriate to them. We become aware of the causes that have led to this new life and realize their justice.

The preview was also reported by Whitton's subjects as a "planning" session, in which the incarnating self cooperates consciously in working out the overall pattern of the coming life. This concept is significant, for it implies that we are more than helpless victims of a reincarnational process. We also have some responsibility for arranging it.

The mechanism by which an individual is actually brought into a new birth must be a complex operation of natural laws. Some of Whitton's subjects give accounts in which they were personally engaged in the process of choosing a body, an impression also created by *The Tibetan Book of the Dead*, but such accounts read like after-the-fact descriptions trying to express the unfamiliar in familiar terms. The theosophical tradition talks about allegorical figures called "Lipikas," the scribes or recorders of karma, who are connected with the birth and destiny of every child. Clairvoyants like C. W. Leadbeater and Geoffrey Hodson have seen personified forces of nature, the "elementals," involved in the process. All these descriptions may be more or less allegorical expressions for different aspects of the same natural process.

Conception and Moral Issues

The precise moment when the essential self makes contact with its new body is unclear. The question is of some importance for the issue of abortion, for to abort a fetus that has no essential self associated with it would be no more serious morally than snipping off an unwanted appendix. But to abort one which an essential self had already entered into would be to interfere with the life plan of that other self and indeed of one's own karma. It would be killing.

Unfortunately for easy moral stances, how an essential self gets associated with a developing new body and what it means for that self to "enter into" the new body are themselves complex questions. It is said that the connection between self and body is usually made at the moment of conception, when the sperm and the egg unite to produce the zygote from which the fetus develops. That would mean that abortion at any stage is depriving the self of a life expression—is killing.

However, it is also said that the essential self often identifies its prospective parents before conception and waits for conception to occur. Logically, that would mean that any reluctance to conceive, whether by the use of birth control techniques or simply by abstention from sexual relations, is likewise denying a bodily form to a self seeking reincarnation. Looked at that way, there is no clear ethical difference between frustrating reincarnation before or after conception. However, hardly anyone would suggest that therefore all fertile men and women should devote themselves to bringing as many bodies into existence as possible.

On the other hand, it is also said that the essential self cannot enter fully into incarnation, that is, take complete charge of its body, until sometime around the seventh year of life. A critical point in childhood, this age is widely accepted as the "age of reason," when children begin to be held morally responsible for their actions. An argument could be mounted—although most of us would reject it vigorously as spurious—that because the essential self is not in full possession of its body until after the seventh year, the murder of infants is less culpable than the murder of adults, or even that the abandonment of unwanted babies is morally permissible. Indeed, there have been cultures, and still are, in which abandoning children in the wilderness is accepted. Greek and Roman legend has several examples of it.

A difficulty in basing moral judgments on the biological and psychological facts of reincarnation is that the process of incarnation does not seem to be a simple one. The "soul" does not suddenly fall into a body. Rather there is a tentative connection made between a self that wants to incarnate and a situation—not even necessarily a body yet, but only the potential for a body. Then the process by which the self identifies with and enters (in some sense) into the new body is a protracted one. It is achieved slowly by degrees.

The process of an incarnation may be frustrated—delayed or blocked—at various stages and in various ways. In such cases, the incarnating self must wait or seek other opportunities. The dividing line between morally permissible and impermissible interference in another self's process of incarnation is not given by nature. It is a human decision. We cannot absolve ourselves of the necessity of making such moral decisions by citing supposed facts about reincarnation.

This is not to say that the concept of reincarnation is irrelevant to the question of abortion (or other moral issues, like capital punishment or war). It is very relevant. But it does not obviate the need for each of us to come to grips with these ethical issues ourselves. Indeed, looking upon the inner or hidden side of life affects our view of almost everything about it. The very act of conception may involve more on the hidden side of life than it does on the external.

THE INNER SIDE OF CONCEPTION

When a man and woman join in sexual union, more than their physical bodies are coupled. In addition to the physical joining, there is an interflow of vital energies, a merging of emotions, a combining of thoughts, and sometimes even a uniting of intuitional ideals. The male and the female are complementary in their sexual polarity not only in their physical forms, but on all levels of their personal being.

We can imagine sexual union as therefore producing a swirling, intertwining rush of forces and energies on all the inner levels. This intertwining of opposite polarities on a variety of levels of being creates a powerful spiritual magnet that draws to it other forces and energies of a comparable kind. And in the process it may draw to it essential selves who are ready to be reborn and who have a need for the hereditary and environmental circumstances afforded by the couple. Or, as suggested earlier, some essential self may already be linked to the prospective parents and be waiting only for the occasion to enter into life through them.

Just as only one sperm normally enters an egg, whose surface immediately becomes impermeable to other sperm seeking entry, so normally only one essential self succeeds in making contact with the fertilized egg that the coupling produces. Once the connection between incarnating self and the incipient fetus has been made, a psychic impermeability refuses entry to any others who may have been seeking that birth. An exception is the case of identical twins, in which two essential selves karmically require the same heredity and environment.

LIGHT, WORD, ROLE, AND ATOM

However the contact is made, it consists of the essential self sending part of itself into the developing new entity. The language used about this event is likely to mislead us. It is not as though a fragment of the essential self were broken off and dunked into matter, like a piece of bread from a loaf to sop up gravy. There are better metaphors for the process.

Light. It is rather as though the essential self is a powerful flame that sends out a single concentrated ray. That ray lights up the object it falls upon and by the concentrated strength of its energies produces changes in the object. Just as a ray of sunlight, concentrated by a lens, can cause a pile of wood shavings to catch fire, so the ray from the essential self causes the matter of the body it enters into to catch fire—with vitality and feeling and cognizance.

Our personal self is a fire that has been kindled by the power of the light shining into our body from the flame of our essential self. That too is a metaphor and must not be pushed too far, but it suggests something of the relationship between the enduring essential self, the "real" us, and the transitory personal self, with which we identify in our everyday life.

Word. Another metaphor, based on vibration and sound, can be used for the process of incarnation. In the Wisdom Tradition, the world is said to be created by sound, the utterance of a word. Genesis describes the creative act as the Elohim speaking: "Let there be light!" The Gospel according to John, drawing on Neoplatonic and gnostic sources, says, "In the beginning was the Word."

The Hindu tradition says that the primal differentiation of the Absolute is *Vach*, the Voice. The world is the Word made material. It is sound frozen as substance. The concept of matter as a form of vibration is one with which present-day physics is increasingly comfortable.

Since analogy holds between things great and small, human life can be seen also as an expression of sound. The essential self is a word—our true name. When it wishes to incarnate, its vibration is echoed forth in the denser worlds of matter, on another octave, as it were, setting up harmonic vibrations, by which it expresses itself in those worlds. Our physical body is the effect of that vibration in this world. Our whole incarnated personal self is a chord based on the fundamental tone of our essential self.

Role. Yet another metaphor is derived from the stage. In *As You Like It*, one of Shakespeare's characters, Jacques, says:

> . . .All the world's a stage,
> And all the men and women merely players.
> They have their exits and their entrances,
> And one man in his time plays many parts,
> His acts being seven ages.

The essential self in us is like an actor who assumes a role. We dress the part. We "psych up" ourselves so that we identify with the role we are playing, as any good actor must if the performance is to be successful. For the duration of the performance, we are the character we represent—we become the role.

While we are playing a particular part, we banish from the forefront of our minds all recollection of our real lives and of all other roles we have played in the past. It would not do for us to walk onto the stage preoccupied with the facts of our real life—with concerns about paying bills and meeting friends for dinner. No more would it do to remember the lines and character of Lady Bracknell in Oscar Wilde's *Importance of Being Earnest* if we are playing the drug-addicted mother in Eugene O'Neill's *Long Day's Journey into Night*. We must not confuse a brittle, sophisticated character in a comedy of manners with a tormented, tragic character in a psychological drama. During the performance of the play, we must enter wholly into the dramatic world of the play.

Similarly, our essential self is an actor who takes on

many and diverse roles—now woman, now man; now rich, now poor; now obscure, now influential; now one race, now another. We are not any of those roles or personalities. But while we are assuming a given personality-role, we must do so whole-heartedly, completely, convincingly. We must convince even ourselves that we are the person we are playing; otherwise the performance would fail. When the curtain falls, however, we take off the costume, we remove the greasepaint, we re-become our real selves until it is time to put on a new play. Then we must learn the new lines, develop the new character, and finally enter the theater and start our new performance.

Atom and Bead. Yet another description of the process of incarnation is more literal in impression. It says that the essential self has, or even is, a kind of "thread" to which are attached five permanent or seed atoms, like beads on a string. These are not "atoms" as present-day scientists use that term, but rather vibratory capacities that are basic to various levels of reality.

For each level of reality on which the essential self functions, there is one atom of the matter of that level which is permanently associated with the essential self. In the vibratory possibilities of these permanent atoms are stored all the capabilities the essential self has developed through past experiences on that level. Thus each of us has a permanent atom on each of the physical, the emotional, and the mental levels of reality.

When the essential self is between incarnations and therefore is not functioning in the physical, emotional, and mental worlds, its permanent atoms of those worlds are dormant. When the essential self comes back into incarnation, it draws to itself and activates its permanent atom in each world, using them as the seeds from which the full bodies are constructed.

The permanent atom functions like the seed molecule

of a crystaline substance in a solution—the solution will crystalize around it. So the unique vibration of the permanent or seed atoms gives a characteristic stamp to the bodies built up around them. These atoms, then, are the link between lives, the carriers of influence from one life to the next. They are an explanation of how the skandhas operate.

All through life, the permanent atom remains within the body through which the essential self functions. Its vibration has determined the character of that body, but in turn the experiences of each lifetime modify the way the permanent atom vibrates. At death, when the body is abandoned by the intelligence operating through it and decomposes, the permanent atom goes into a state of quiescence, waiting to be activated when the self to which it is connected next appears in its world and builds a new body of its matter.

Metaphor and Reality. All these metaphors and presumed descriptions are efforts to state the relationship between our personal identity and that part of us which survives the death of each body, linking lifetime to lifetime. They are efforts to picture how it is that our immortal core takes on mortality and comes into the transitory world of living and dying. We are a light shining in the darkness, imparting fire to the otherwise inert substance of the personality. We are a word, a sound uttered in the silence, echoing through the worlds and the ages. We are an actor playing many parts. We are a string of beads, the permanent atoms, around which the personality crystalizes.

The Irish poet William Butler Yeats said, "Eternity is in love with the productions of Time." In our essential self, we are that Eternity. In our personal selves, we are those productions of Time. The one begets the other, however we symbolize the process, because a powerful force—call it love, desire, or longing—impels us into activity. We are all makers, as J. R. R. Tolkien said, because we are made. It is our nature to produce, as we were produced. By our act of making, we participate in the creative act of the universe, and what we make is ourselves.

12

Why Do We Reincarnate?

Why ever do we do it? What's the meaning of it all? What is the purpose of reincarnation?

It is inevitable that we should ask such questions if we take reincarnation seriously. Of course, the answer may be that there is no reason—that it is just the way the world is. But human beings have seldom been satisfied with such an answer. We expect there to be a reason for everything. The Gospel of John starts "In the beginning was the Word," but the Greek term translated "Word" also means "Reason." We insist that in the beginning, at the basis of things, there should be a reason for everything.

In the theosophical tradition, the reason for reincarnation is to further human evolution, specifically the evolution of the human mind, for there is intellectual and spiritual evolution as well as the evolution of physical forms. Through reincarnation we develop our understanding of the universe and of our place in it. Our destiny is to become fully what we are now only potentially—centers of the authentic life, wisdom, and creativity of the ground of all being.

Theosophy teaches that there is only one ultimate reality in the universe, of which all apparently separate beings are temporary expressions. Human beings, stars,

amebas, swirling galaxies, and subatomic particles—
all are emanations from the one reality through which
it realizes its being, comes to know itself, and expresses
its creative nature. Reincarnation is part of the cosmic
process by which the many come forth from and finally return to the One.

Because it regards reincarnation as part of a cosmic
and purposeful evolutionary process, Theosophy has a
basically optimistic attitude toward life in the world and
our repeated reincarnations in it. We reincarnate to
learn the lessons that life has for us, to participate joyous
ly in the process of creation, and to express in a small
but essential way the nature of ultimate being. When
we have done that, we will have passed beyond the need
to reincarnate, a process that is admittedly often a painful one.

Two Attitudes toward the World

In general there are two attitudes toward the role of
reincarnation in our larger lives. One sees us as basically spiritual beings who have slipped into the world of
matter, which is a singularly uncomfortable place to be.
We strive to free ourselves from the pain and limitations
of this world, but are seldom successful. Reincarnation
is the process by which we keep slipping back into the
mire of physical reality.

According to this attitude, we need to get out of the
world, to free ourselves from its pain and sorrow—and
hence from the need to reincarnate. This attitude regards
the physical world pessimistically and so is world-
denying.

The other view sees us as composite beings, part matter, part consciousness—or perhaps more accurately, a
correlation between matter and consciousness, a synthesis of the two. As such, we exist only because we are

in the world. And being in the world is our way of coming to be.

According to this attitude, we create our own natures by defining ourselves as we interact with the world. We are not a soul that dresses up in a body, like a suit of woolens. Rather we are what happens when consciousness tries to get to know itself by reaching out into the world. This is a basically optimistic attitude that celebrates the physical world and affirms it.

The two attitudes can also be seen in what Buddhism and Hinduism (at least in two of their forms) have to say about the ultimate nature of experience. The Buddha taught that our experience of this world reveals three characteristics of it: no-selfness, impermanence, and frustration *(anatta, anicca, dukkha)*. That is, nothing in the world has a core identity, a permanent self or soul; everything is a composite of fluctuating elements. Because nothing has an abiding central core, all things change constantly—nothing remains the same from one moment to the next; there is no stability. Since we human beings long for stability and permanence, we are constantly frustrated by the changing kaleidoscope around us. Life, then, is a very unsatisfactory affair, consisting of unreality, darkness, and death.

In Hinduism, on the other hand, there is a teaching that the nature of ultimate reality is threefold: being, awareness, and joy *(sat, chit, ananda)*. In the universe there is one being only, one reality, one Self; all the other beings that appear in manifold variety throughout the universe are merely partial and temporary expressions of that one Being. The one Being is endowed with an awareness of itself, and that awareness encompasses in a single act of knowing all the apparent variety and change throughout the whole of the cosmos. The one Being's awareness of its own unity behind all appearances gives rise to joyous creativity. In this view, the cosmos is ultimately an expression of reality, light, and immortality.

These two attitudes, although seemingly so different, are in fact complementary to each other. The first is about a fragmented state of consciousness, and the second is about a unified state. The first is about our isolated experience of physical limitations, and the second is about a vision of the harmony of the Whole. The Hindu scriptures have a mantra or prayer:

> From the unreal lead us to the real.
> From darkness lead us to light.
> From death lead us to immortality.
> Peace unto all the world.

Reincarnation is part of the evolutionary spiral that leads us from one state of being to the other. In the process, we need both views of the world.

The first attitude, taken alone, may lead to a debilitating sense of pessimism and despair. The second, taken alone, may produce a facile sense of optimism that is easily broken by the hard and painful realities of life. Schopenhauer and the existentialists veered toward the first. Voltaire made fun of the second in his satire *Candide*, in which the hero passes through the most dreadful experiences imaginable, remembering his teacher Pangloss's affirmation that this is "the best of all possible worlds."

In reality, the two attitudes are saying the same thing, but from different points of view. There are no core selves in the things of this world because there is only one Self in the universe. There is constant change in all things; awareness requires the contrast produced by change and cannot exist without change. Frustration and joy, tension and release, are two sides of the same experience. So too, the purpose of reincarnation is to teach us everything we have to learn in this world, and thereby

make it unnecessary to return to the world. The need
for reincarnation and the hope to escape from reincarnation imply each other.

The difference between the pessimistic and the optimistic attitudes toward life is one of viewpoint. It has
been said that an optimist is one who believes that this
is the best of all possible worlds, and a pessimist is one
who is afraid the optimist is right. Or, as an old adver-
tising slogan for a chain of doughnut shops put it:

> As you travel on through life, brother,
> Whatever be your goal,
> Keep your eye upon the doughnut,
> And not upon the hole.

How we regard reincarnation will depend on whether
we look at the doughnut or at the hole.

EVOLUTION AND REINCARNATION

The theosophical attitude toward reincarnation is that
it, like everything else in the universe, has a place in
the cosmic order. Rebirth is not just a matter of one life
after another. It serves a purpose. It has an end. And
that end is to further evolution. In the theosophical tradition, evolution is not a blind, meaningless response to
causes. It also has a purpose: to increase the quality of
being, of awareness, and of joy.

Theosophically speaking, evolution is more than just
the process by which the various species of animals and
plants have developed out of earlier forms by a mutation of their genes through the ages. It includes that,
but is more. Evolution is, to use the words of a Merriam-
Webster dictionary, "a process in which the whole universe is a progression of interrelated phenomena."

The universal process of evolution involves, according

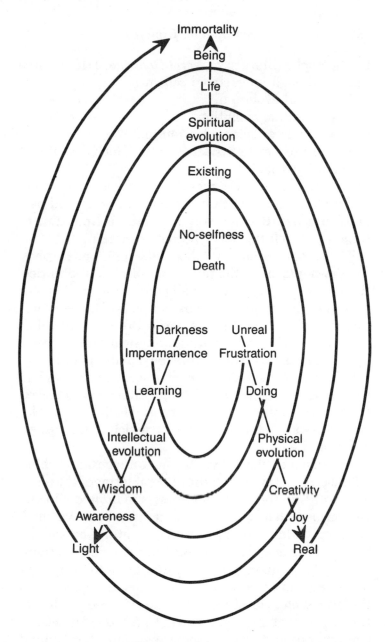

SPIRAL OF EVOLUTION

to Theosophy (Blavatsky, *Secret Doctrine*, 1:181), three distinct though interrelated schemes:
1. Physical evolution.
2. Intellectual evolution.
3. Monadic or spiritual evolution.

The first scheme, physical evolution, includes the sort of evolution scientists are concerned with. It involves competition among the members of a species for food and mates, with the fittest surviving to breed and pass on their genes. It also involves mutations from time to time, by which the genes become different.

The second scheme, intellectual evolution, involves the development of the mind and of mental abilities. Reincarnation applies especially to this aspect of evolution. Indeed, reincarnation has a function in the evolution of consciousness that is parallel to the survival of the fittest in physical evolution. Physical forms survive by being fit and therefore able to feed abundantly and breed freely. Nonphysical consciousness also survives and progresses by being fit—but its fitness is achieved through extending its experience as widely as possible. Reincarnation is the technique by which consciousness grows and adapts.

According to Blavatsky, the one consciousness behind all life pushes its way into the mineral forms of the physical world. In them consciousness is so limited and circumscribed that we speak of it as atomic valence, chemical affinity, response to temperature, crystalization, or fatigue and hardly recognize it as consciousness at all. After a quantum-leap mutation in the way consciousness can express itself, it appears in vegetation as impulses such as growth, flowering and seeding, leaves turning to light and roots to water. Another quantum-leap mutation takes consciousness into the animal kingdom, where we recognize it as something familiar to us. And yet another such mutation produces the hominid kingdom, where self-reflection, language, and speculative imagination are the hallmarks of consciousness.

Beyond humanity we can imagine still more complex and aware varieties of consciousness. For certainly our kind of conscious life is not the apex of evolution. It may be the highest most of us are aware of, but the amount of our knowledge is as nothing compared to the vastness of our ignorance. As Hamlet told his friend, "There are more things in heaven and earth, Horatio, than are dreamt of in your philosophy." According to Theosophy, evolution will not stop with us. Beyond humanity there must be superhumanity, and reincarnation leads toward it.

The third scheme of evolution, the monadic, is something about which we can say very little. It lies in the future with that superhumanity. Intellectual evolution cannot progress very far until physical evolution has developed the appropriate forms to express intellect. Similarly, monadic evolution cannot get underway significantly until intellectual evolution has produced a mind that can contain and reflect the inner glory of the monad —that unit of intuitive wisdom and ultimate Self. Our minds, though developing, are still a long way from being adequate vehicles to express the fullness of the monad. As Blavatsky put it:

> Therefore, the Kabalists say correctly that "MAN becomes a stone, a plant, an animal, a man, a Spirit, and finally God. Thus accomplishing his cycle or circuit and returning to the point from which he had started as the *heavenly* MAN." But by "Man" the divine Monad is meant, and not the thinking Entity, much less his physical body. (*Secret Doctrine* 2:186)

In each of the great stages of evolution, there is reincarnation of a type, although the type must obviously differ radically between minerals, plants, animals, and human beings. At one extreme, the very substance of matter, the subatomic particles, blink off and on in a fantastic dance of death and reincarnation. In the human stage of evolution, reincarnation produces and develops the individuality, the core or essential self that binds one personal life to another through the centuries and eons.

In the long run, that essential self is not permanent either—there being no ultimately permanent selves other than the one Self. But during a short time span (still long to us), our individual selves provide a continuing link between one personal life and the next. That individuality is both the means by which reincarnation works and its purpose.

The End of Reincarnation

One aim of reincarnation is to develop the individual self as completely as possible, to build it up and release its potential through a vast series of personal lives or incarnations. Reincarnation is the means by which we make ourselves, by which we become fully individual.

The evolution of our individual consciousness is a do-it-yourself job. There may be patterns to follow and assistants to show us the way. But finally we have to do it ourselves—each of us alone. Yet each of us is in the company of others engaged in the same quest. Our pilgrimage is no solitary journey. We travel in a great company and with well-known companions.

When the individual self has been developed fully, when we are completely individuated, the next quantum leap will doubtless carry us beyond individuality to a state of conscious interrelatedness and wholeness. As we build up our individual selves through reincarnation, we also establish those links and contacts with one another that will one day in the distant evolutionary future provide the quantum leap that takes us out of humanity into superhumanity.

Evolution does not proceed in hermetically sealed compartments. There are overlaps, links between the kingdoms. A virus is a little like a molecule and a little like a microorganism. A chimpanzee is a little like a monkey and a little like a human being. So too, even now we can catch glimpses of a superhumanity which lives in interrelated wholeness. There have been perfected human beings among us—few in number but powerful in effect, the spiritual leaders of our species. The purpose of reincarnation is to make us what they are.

When that purpose has been fulfilled, reincarnation will become something radically different from what it now is. The kind of reincarnation we now experience, the dipping down into the physical world to develop a series of personal selves, will end, and be replaced by some other kind of cyclical experience that we cannot even imagine. Then we will be born no more. For reincarnation will have fulfilled its ultimate purpose, which is to make itself unnecessary. The end of reincarnation is to overcome the need for reincarnation. But that end is still a long way down the road for most of us. What we can do in the meanwhile is enjoy the process. Half the fun, they say, is getting there.

In a sense, the whole process of manifestation—the coming forth of the monad from the ultimate Oneness and its return to it—is a single grand incarnation. It is succeeded by other similar incarnations in vast evolutionary cycles. For reincarnation is the pattern of the universe, of which our little personal incarnations are only minor cycles.

Yet those minor cycles, our reincarnation as successive personalities, also fill their role in the cosmic economy. And that role is to increase the quality of our being, awareness, and joy. Through reincarnation we come to rejoice in the world. Through reincarnation we learn all that is to be learned. Through reincarnation we develop into complete beings.

From the frustration of these lives, joy will sprout. From the impermanence of these lives, awareness will grow. From the no-selfness of these lives, truly unselfish Being will flower. That is the purpose of reincarnation. That is its end.

APPENDIX

Terms for Reincarnation and Allied Concepts

*E*nglish has a number of terms for reincarnation and related concepts:

1. *Reincarnation,* the commonest term, was introduced into English in the middle of the nineteenth century. It is built up of five Latin elements: *re-* 'again,' *in-* 'into,' *carn* 'flesh,' *-ate* 'cause or become,' and *-ion* 'process.' And so it means literally 'the process of coming into flesh again.'

2. *Rebirth* is the simplest term. It would be the best one to use, except for the fact that it is ambiguous, having several meanings. Most particularly it is used by some Christians to refer to an experience of spiritual renewal.

3. *Transmigration,* another word derived from Latin, has been in English since the sixteenth century. It is built of *trans-* 'across,' *migr-* 'to go or move,' and *-ation* 'process of causing or becoming.' Its literal sense is something like 'the process of going across'—across the realm of death into another body. The term is sometimes used to include the possibility of humans being reborn as animals, which the theosophical tradition says does not occur.

133

4. *Metempsychosis* is another sixteenth century word, formed however from Greek elements: *meta-* 'later, beyond, changed,' *em-* or *en-* 'into,' *psyche* 'soul,' and *-osis* 'process.' It is thus 'the process by which the soul gets changed after (death) into (a new body).'

5. *Metensomatosis* is a similar, but rarer, word also from Greek elements (some the same as those above): *meta-, en-, soma(t)* 'body,' and *-osis*. It is literally 'the process of coming back into a body' or 'reembodiment.'

6. *Palingenesis* is a nineteenth century English word based on Greek elements: *palin* 'back, again' and *genesis* 'origin, birth.' Thus it literally means 'being born again, rebirth.'

7. *Serial life* or *serial consciousness* is a recent term used to suggest that any given lifetime is merely one in a series of events. It is a less pretentious term than some of the classically derived ones. It also leaves unspecified the form of connection between the lives in a series but emphasizes their relative independence.

Some of those terms are mouth-filling, but they all mean at least approximately the same thing. A number of other terms that one occasionally meets denote different, though related concepts:

8. *Preexistence* is the belief that we existed before we were born in our present bodies. Reincarnation implies preexistence since, if we will have future lives, we certainly also have had past ones. But some people have believed that the soul exists before its birth, not in other bodies in this world, but rather in some other realm of existence, so preexistence is not necessarily the same thing as reincarnation.

9. *Metamorphosis* means transformation, and refers to a change of physical form during one lifetime, as when a caterpillar becomes a butterfly.

10. *Eternal return* or *recurrence* denotes an idea of the German philosopher Friedrich Nietzsche that every-

thing that now exists has existed before and will exist again in exactly the same way—that the world repeats itself precisely. His argument is that, if the world consists of a finite (even though very large) number of atoms, then there is also a finite number of arrangements for them. Although the atoms are in constant flux, they must in the course of endless time finally repeat their earlier arrangements. So the world as we know it now must have existed before and will exist again in exactly the same form. In effect we relive our same lives in every detail.

Bibliography

Bernstein, Morey. *The Search for Bridey Murphy*. Garden City, N.Y.: Doubleday, 1956. Reprint, New York: Lancer, 1965. Reprint, New York: Pocket Books, 1978.

Besant, Annie. *Death--and After*. Theosophical Manual no. 3. Adyar, Madras, India: Theosophical Pub. House, 1952 and earlier.

———. *The Necessity for Reincarnation*. Adyar, Madras, India: Theosophical Pub. House, 1978, 1920.

———. *Popular Lectures on Theosophy*. 2nd ed. Adyar, Madras, India: Theosophist Office, 1912. 1st ed. 1910.

———. *Reincarnation*. Theosophical Manual no. 2. Adyar, Madras, India: Theosophical Pub House, 1970, 1892.

Blavatsky, H. P. *The Key to Theosophy*. 3d ed. London: Theosophical Pub. Soc., 1893.

———. *The Secret Doctrine: The Synthesis of Science, Religion, and Philosophy*. 2 vols. London: Theosophical Pub. Co., 1888.

Cerminara, Gina. *The World Within*. New York: William Sloane, 1957.

Challoner, H. K. *The Wheel of Rebirth: An Autobiography of Many Lifetimes*. Wheaton, Ill.: Theosophical Pub. House, 1976, c. 1969.

Cooper, Irving S. *Reincarnation: A Hope of the World*. Wheaton, Ill.: Theosophical Pub. House, 1979. 1st ed. 1918, as *Reincarnation: The Hope of the World*.

Cranston, Sylvia, and Carey Williams. *Reincarnation: A New Horizon in Science, Religion, and Society.* New York: Julian, 1984.

Evans-Wentz, W. Y. *The Tibetan Book of the Dead.* London: Oxford Univ. Press, 1960.

Farthing, Geoffrey A. *Exploring the Great Beyond.* Wheaton, Ill.: Theosophical Pub. House, 1978.

————. *When We Die.* London: Theosophical Pub. House, 1968.

Fisher, Joe. *The Case for Reincarnation.* Preface by the Dalai Lama. Toronto: Bantam, 1985 (1984).

Gallup, George, Jr., with William Proctor. *Adventures in Immortality.* London: Corgi, 1982.

Gardner, E. L. *Reincarnation: Some Testimony from Nature.* London: Theosophical Society in England, 1965.

Grey, Margot. *Return from Death: An Exploration of the Near-Death Experience.* London: Arkana, 1985.

Grof, Stanislav, and Joan Halifax. *The Human Encounter with Death.* New York: Dutton, 1977.

Guirdham, Arthur. *The Cathars and Reincarnation.* Wheaton, Ill.: Theosophical Pub. House, 1978. 1st pub. 1970.

Hall, Manly P. *Death to Rebirth.* Los Angeles: Philosophical Research Soc., 1979.

————. *Reincarnation: The Cycle of Necessity.* Los Angeles: Philosophical Research Soc., 1978. 1st pub. 1939.

————. *Research on Reincarnation.* Los Angeles: Philosophical Research Soc., 1964.

Hampton, Charles. *Reincarnation: A Christian Doctrine.* Los Angeles: St. Albans Press, 1925.

————. *The Transition Called Death: A Recurring Experience.* Wheaton, Ill.: Theosophical Pub. House, 1979. Earlier pub. as *Transition* with an extra chapter on "War Victims and Reincarnation." Adyar, Madras, India: Theosophical Pub. House, 1943.

Hartley, Christine. *A Case for Reincarnation.* London: Robert Hale, 1972.

Haynes, Renée. *The Society for Psychical Research, 1882-1982: A History.* London: Macdonald, 1982.

Head, Joseph, and S. L. Cranston, eds. *Reincarnation in World Thought: A Living Study of Reincarnation in All Ages; Including Selections from the World's Religions, Philosophies and Sciences, and Great Thinkers of the Past and Present.* New York: Julian, 1967.

——. *Reincarnation: An East-West Anthology, Including Quotations from the World's Religions and from Over 400 Western Thinkers.* Wheaton, Ill.: Theosophical Pub. House, 1975, 1968, 1st pub. 1961.

——. *Reincarnation, The Phoenix Fire Mystery: An East-West Dialogue on Death and Rebirth from the Worlds of Religion, Science, Psychology, Philosophy, Art, and Literature, and from Great Thinkers of the Past and Present.* New York: Julian Press/Crown Publishers, 1977.

Hick, John. *Death and Eternal Life.* San Francisco: Harper & Row, 1976.

Hodson, Geoffrey. *The Miracle of Birth: A Clairvoyant Study of a Human Embryo.* Wheaton, Ill.: Theosophical Pub. House, 1981.

——. *Reincarnation: Fact or Fallacy? An Examination and Exposition of the Doctrine of Rebirth.* Wheaton, Ill.: Theosophical Pub. House, 1972, 1967, revised ed.; orig. pub. 1951.

Howe, Quincy, Jr. *Reincarnation for the Christian.* Philadelphia: Westminster Press, 1974. Reissued, Wheaton, Ill.: Theosophical Pub. House, 1987.

Humphreys, Christmas. *Karma and Rebirth.* London: John Murray, 1943.

Iverson, Jeffrey. *More Lives than One?* New York: Warner, 1976.

Jinarajadasa, C. *How We Remember Our Past Lives and Other Essays on Reincarnation.* Adyar, Madras, India: Theosophical Pub. House, 1915.

Johnston, Charles. *The Memory of Past Births.* New York: Theosophical Soc. Pub. Dept., 1899.

Kelsey, Denys, and Joan Grant. *Many Lifetimes.* Garden City, N.Y.: Doubleday, 1967.

Langley, Noel. *Edgar Cayce on Reincarnation.* Ed. Hugh Lynn Cayce. New York: Warner Books, 1967.

Lati Rinbochay and Jeffrey Hopkins. *Death, Intermediate State and Rebirth in Tibetan Buddhism.* Foreword by Dalai Lama. Valois, N.Y.: Gabriel/Snow Lion, 1980, 1979.

Leadbeater, C. W. *The Astral Plane: Its Scenery, Inhabitants, and Phenomena.* 3d ed. London: Theosophical Pub. Soc., 1900.

————. *The Devachanic Plane; or, The Heaven World: Its Characteristics and Inhabitants.* 2d ed. London: Theosophical Pub. Soc., 1902.

————. *Invisible Helpers.* 1st Indian ed., rev. and enlarged. Adyar, Madras, India: Theosophical Pub. House, 1928.

————. *The Life after Death and How Theosophy Unveils It.* Adyar, Madras, India: Theosophical Pub. House, 1952.

————. *The Other Side of Death.* 2nd ed. Adyar, Madras, India: Theosophical Pub. House, 1928.

————. *The Soul's Growth through Reincarnation: Lives of Erato and Spica.* 4 vols. Ed. C. Jinarajadasa. Adyar, Madras, India: Theosophical Pub. House, 1941, 1946, 1948, 1950.

Lenz, Frederick. *Lifetimes: True Accounts of Reincarnation.* Indianapolis: Bobbs-Merrill, 1979.

Lorimer, David. *Survival? Body, Mind and Death in the Light of Psychic Experience.* London: Routledge & Kegan Paul, 1984.

Luntz, Charles E. *The Challenge of Reincarnation.* Foreword by Morey Bernstein. St. Louis: Charles E. Luntz, 1957.

MacGregor, Geddes. *Reincarnation as a Christian Hope.* London: Macmillan, 1982.

————. *Reincarnation in Christianity: A New Vision of the Role of Rebirth in Christian Thought.* Wheaton, Ill.: Theosophical Pub. House, 1978.

MacLaine, Shirley. *Dancing in the Light.* New York: Bantam, 1985.

————. *Out on a Limb.* New York: Bantam, 1983, reprint, 1984, 1986.

The Mahatma Letters to A. P. Sinnett from the Mahatmas M. & K.H. Ed. A. T. Barker. 3rd ed. Christmas Humphreys and Elsie Benjamin. Adyar, Madras, India: Theosophical Pub. House, 1962.

Marsh, Michael. *A Matter of Personal Survival: Life after Death.* Wheaton, Ill.: Theosophical Pub. House, 1985.

Martin, Eva, ed. *The Ring of Return: An Anthology of References to Reincarnation and Spiritual Evolution from Prose and Poetry of All Ages.* London: Philip Allan, 1927. Reprint, as *Reincarnation: The Ring of Return.* New Hyde Park, N.Y.: University Books, 1963.

Moody, Raymond A., Jr. *Life after Life: The Investigation of a Phenomenon—Survival of Bodily Death.* Intro. Elisabeth Kubler-Ross. Harrisburg, Pa.: Stackpole, 1976.

——. *Reflections on Life after Life.* London: Corgi, 1978. 1st pub. 1977.

O'Flaherty, Wendy Doniger, ed. *Karma and Rebirth in Classical Indian Traditions.* Berkeley and Los Angeles: Univ. of California Press, 1980.

Perkins, James Scudday. *Experiencing Reincarnation.* Wheaton, Ill.: Theosophical Pub. House, 1977.

——. *Through Death to Rebirth.* Wheaton, Ill.: Theosophical Pub. House, 1973, orig. pub. 1961.

Ring, Kenneth. *Life at Death: A Scientific Investigation of the Near-Death Experience.* New York: Coward, McCann & Geoghegan, 1980.

Rogers, L. W. *Reincarnation and Other Lectures.* Chicago: Theo Book Company, 1925.

Rogo, D. Scott. *Life after Death: The Case for Survival of Bodily Death.* Wellingborough, Northamptonshire: Aquarian, 1986.

——. *The Search for Yesterday: A Critical Examination of the Evidence for Reincarnation.* Englewood Cliffs, N.J.: Prentice-Hall, 1985.

Ryall, Edward W. *Born Twice: Total Recall of a Seventeenth-century Life.* Introduction and appendix by Ian Stevenson. New York: Harper & Row, 1974. (Published in England as *Second Time Round.*)

Sabom, Michael B. *Recollections of Death.* London: Corgi, 1982.

Sharma, I. C. *Cayce, Karma & Reincarnation.* Intro. Hugh Lynn Cayce. Wheaton, Ill.: Theosophical Pub. House, 1975, c. 1971.

Smith, E. Lester. *Our Last Adventure: A Commonsense Guide to Death and After*. London: Theosophical Pub. House, 1985.

Stevenson, Ian. *Cases of the Reincarnation Type: Volume I, Ten Cases in India*. Charlottesville: Univ. Press of Virginia, 1975.

———. *Cases of the Reincarnation Type: Volume II, Ten Cases in Sri Lanka*. Charlottesville: Univ. Press of Virginia, 1977.

———. *Cases of the Reincarnation Type: Volume III, Twelve Cases in Lebanon and Turkey*. Charlottesville: Univ. Press of Virginia, 1980.

———. *The Evidence for Survival from Claimed Memories of Former Incarnations*. N.p.: n.p., 1970, 1961. From *Journal of the American Society for Psychical Research* 54 (1960): 51-71, 95-117.

———. *Twenty Cases Suggestive of Reincarnation*. 2d ed., rev. and enlarged. Charlottesville: Univ. Press of Virginia, 1978, 1974, 1st ed. 1966.

———. *Xenoglossy: A Review and Report of a Case*. Bristol: John Wright, 1974. Also as *Proceedings of the American Society for Psychical Research* 31 (1974).

Stewart, R. S. "The Sixth Sense of Alan Jay Lerner." *Atlantic Monthly*, Nov. 1965, 99-102.

Story, Francis. *Rebirth as Doctrine and Experience: Essays and Case Studies*. Intro. Ian Stevenson. Kandy, Sri Lanka: Buddhist Publication Society, 1975.

Thomason, Sarah Grey. "Do You Remember Your Previous Life's Language in Your Present Incarnation?" *American Speech* 59 (1984): 340-50.

Wambach, Helen. *Reliving Past Lives: The Evidence under Hypnosis*. London: Hutchinson, 1979. 1st pub. 1978.

Whitton, Joel L., and Joe Fisher. *Life between Life: Scientific Explorations into the Void Separating One Incarnation from the Next*. London: Grafton (Collins), 1986.

Wilson, Colin. *Afterlife: An Investigation of the Evidence for Life after Death*. London: Harrap, 1985.

Wilson, Ian. *All in the Mind*. Garden City, N.Y.: Doubleday, 1981. Pub. in Britain as *Mind Out of Time? Reincarnation Claims Investigated.* London: Victor Gollancz, 1981.

Wright, Leoline L. *Reincarnation: A Lost Chord in Modern Thought.* With additional chapters by Helen Todd and Steele O'Hara. Wheaton, Ill.: Theosophical Pub. House for Point Loma Publications, 1975.

Index

QUEST BOOKS
are published by
The Theosophical Society in America,
Wheaton, Illinois 60189-0270,
a branch of a world organization
dedicated to the promotion of brotherhood and
the encouragement of the study of religion,
philosophy, and science, to the end that man may
better understand himself and his place in
the universe. The Society stands for complete
freedom of individual search and belief.
In the Classics Series well-known
theosophical works are made
available in popular editions.